MEMOIRS OF A
Working Mother

Fighting for Balance, Managing
Expectations, Channeling Love

LINDA ARREY

13th & Joan
WWW.13THANDJOAN.COM

Memoirs of A Working Mother. Copyright 2018 by Linda Arrey. All rights reserved. No part of this publication may be reproduced, distributed, or transmitted in any form or by any means, including photocopying, recording, or other electronic or mechanical methods, without the prior written permission of the publisher, except in the case of brief quotations embodied in critical reviews and certain other non-commercial uses permitted by copyright law. For permission requests, write to the publisher, addressed "Attention: Permissions Coordinator," 500 N. Michigan Avenue, Suite #600, Chicago, IL 60611.

13th & Joan books may be purchased for educational, business or sales promotional use. For information, please email the Sales Department at sales@13thandjoan.com.

Printed in the U.S. A.

First Printing, June 2018

Library of Congress Cataloging-in-Publication Data has been applied for.

ISBN 978-1-7326464-1-4

MEMOIRS OF A
Working Mother

Ms. Patt,
Thanks for a beautiful day in Delaware. Wishing you much joy, blessings and answered prayers.
be. Linda

PRAISES
FOR MEMOIRS OF A WORKING MOTHER

AS A MOTHER of five, I understand the difficulty of home and work balance. Having spent over sixteen years on active duty with four deployments to combat zones, nursing school and medical school/residency there were many days I lost balance. In "Memoirs of a Working Mother", Linda eloquently captures these struggles and provides insight as to how she fights to maintain balance as an active duty military mom of two beautiful girls and wife to a wonderful husband.

Dr. Kristi Dreyer,
Osteopathic Physician (DO),
Lt Col, Mom of 3 children, 2 stepchildren

BEING A WIFE and working mother of two isn't the easiest job in the world, but it's one of the most rewarding. And in *Memoirs of a Working Mother* Linda has created a safe space for moms to embrace their challenges and celebrate their accomplishments through real-life stories and experiences that many can relate to. Even as everyday superheroes, Linda's candid talk about what moms have to endure in and out of the household shows you that it's perfectly natural and normal to go through the highs and lows of motherhood (with other like-minded moms) who wear invisible capes too.

Lakia Brandenburg, The Wife Coach, Mom of 2

I AM A wife, a working mother of two beautiful children, healthcare professional, nurse educator, speaker, success and culture coach, and author. Having children was a very tedious and challenging journey for me. I was pregnant seven times but only have two children. I had many miscarriages as well as a stillbirth. Despite all the challenges, having the two most beautiful children the world has seen is my most cherished degree. Oh!! how I wish Coach Linda had this book out when I was going through my journey. Her story and journey would have inspired me and assured me that I was not alone. She is creating a forum for women in general to dialogue openly and comfortably about issues that affect work life balance. I suffered from uterine fibroids as well but never talked about it openly. Now, I am in a forum with women who have gone through similar issues, and we can brainstorm together using Linda's tips to find further solutions to the many problems women face daily, while still wearing many other hats. There is a saying, "stories sell while facts tell." Thank you, Linda, for your vision. This book is certainly going to start a movement. I applaud you for sharing your story to empower millions of other women.

Eunice B. Gwanmesia, PhD, MSN, MSHCA, RN, Mom of 2

AS AN OBSTETRICIAN/gynecologist, I have the privilege of hearing all kinds of concerns and issues that plague the working mother. Women want to know how to balance their career yet still be a loving and doting mother and wife. Life happens. If you're not careful, it will zoom by in a blur! Memoirs of a Working Mother gives a face and voice to the concerns of women from all walks of life. We may look different and our paths may be diverse, but at the core, we all have the same goal and desire. We want to be strong, effective, and leave a legacy that will make our children and loved ones proud.

This book is phenomenal. A huge part of its greatness is the fact that the author, International Board Certified Life and Leadership Coach Linda Arrey, is writing from a place of personal experience. She has allowed her tests to become her testimonies so that women everywhere can be encouraged and know that they are not alone. Sometimes, it's difficult to share the hard, personal things with others. From health problems, like fibroids, to managing stress in the workplace. You will find this book will address whatever season of life you are in. You will know that you are not alone.

Pamela R. Lacy, MD

Dedication

DEAR ANGEL | ARIEL,
When I had the first thought of writing this book, I also had thoughts of you. You inspired me to commit the first words to paper the day I felt you move inside of me for the first time. I was reminded that new life was growing within me, listening to my every heartbeat and finding comfort in my warmth.

As the Lord held my hand through two complicated pregnancies, a few things kept me going each time: the day I would be blessed to hear your first cries, the day I would feel you on my bare body, and the day I would feed you your first meals. My hope rested in meeting you face-to-face. My dearest daughters, after nine months, you graced this earth, and you each looked so much like your daddy. As I pen these words, nursing Ariel to sleep, while Angel lays down beside me, head in my lap, I am reminded that you are a part of my body and soul. You came from me. I only existed until you came along. Giving birth to you empowered me to start living. I am thankful that the Lord found me worthy and trusted me enough to make me your mother. Thank you for motivating and inspiring me daily. Thank you for your heartwarming smiles, especially when I pick you up from daycare after a very long day at work. Through you, I see life from a much different perspective, one that makes me an improved version of myself, a better mom, wife, daughter, sibling, and friend. I love you endlessly.

– Mummy

To the mothers of the world, always remember that you have what it takes. You are enough. You have the greatest gift that your children will ever need – LOVE.

FOREWORD
GIVE. NURTURE. INFLUENCE.

FROM THE BEGINNING of time, women have personified fluency in their ability to balance. The compelling process of giving life to the world epitomizes the woman's ability to impart balance. As women, we are capable of holding the weight of the world on our shoulders. From conception throughout the growth of the baby in the womb, we balance life for more than just ourselves. It is our divine appointment to ensure that all is right in the world. With conviction, we bear the burden of motherhood with dignity, pride and effortless beauty. From mothers who are still working forty hours a week executing all of their responsibilities associated with everyday life to mothers who weather the storms of difficult pregnancies, all manage to find strength to sustain. Women were made to thrive at every level and to give of themselves freely. The word motherhood is synonymous with balance. God has allowed us to carry and bring forth the greatest gift conceptualized: human life. Even after the immense pain that is endured, we bring forth the most profound reward and it is a miraculous wonder!

There is no question that women are a phenom. In our society and culture in general, we are the backbone of existence. We are born to nurture the world and to impart change that makes the world better. We are responsible for the cultivation of generations. With great responsibility, we've proven ourselves to be both resilient and resourceful. A woman has the ability to turn any situation that resembles a challenge into a triumph. It is my belief that women have this discerning capability more than the male counterpart, who have been blessed with their own respective qualities. The proof is in the countless generations of women that make up our existence and their vast history of accomplishments.

We are genetically prone to give, nurture, and influence. It is in the midst of this divine purpose that we feel fulfilled. In all of our doing, we must remember to give, nurture, and influence ourselves. We must never forget to feed our minds, bodies, and souls to continue to balance all that is demanded of us at a steady pace. Life is a marathon, not a sprint. We must also remember not to lose ourselves in motherhood. There is a beautiful soul with hopes, dreams, and ambitions living inside of us who is tasked with balancing her own wants, needs and desires with the charge of raising healthy, happy people to inhabit the world.

All roads of motherhood lead to potential. As women, we unleash and cultivate potential and opportunity into the world. On a daily basis, I am blessed to bear witness to the greatest embodiment of potential as new life enters the world. I often wonder if I'm delivering the first female president or a child gifted to go to outer space. What will this little life accomplish for the greater good of mankind? The possibilities are endless. I am amazed at the potential of one little seed which is the crux of what we nurture and influence. The world as we know it would not bear fruit, if it were not for God's blessing to women. I challenge you to learn to live life in the moment and to enjoy the gifts of its labor. Although motherhood is no easy task, it is a gift to be unwrapped on a daily basis. To be a mother is to personify love. In the end, Love is all we need to endure the tests and trials of life.

— Pamela R. Lacy, MD

PREFACE
DISCOVER LOVE

*Having a baby is like falling
in love for the first time.*
Linda Arrey

IN 2015, I traveled with my husband to the UK. We knew that we now wanted to start a family. I purchased an ovulation kit. I knew that because he worked in the UK, our only opportunities to conceive were when I was in the UK with him or when he was at home with me. As fate would have it, every time I peed on the stick, it was negative. It appeared that I wasn't ovulating. I knew that if I didn't get pregnant, we would try again, immediately. In my mind, I knew that we should not stress because eventually, it would happen, but I couldn't help but be a little anxious.

We did not want to pressure ourselves to the point that making love became robotic. It stops being pleasurable in those moments. Eventually, I stopped placing emphasis on the ovulation kit.

When my husband returned to work in Europe, I can remember calling one day to tell him: "My period came."

Later, the nature of bleeding led me to believe that it was implantation bleeding. I made the decision to purchase a pregnancy kit, and took a home pregnancy test. The result was positive. I was filled with a series of emotions. My girlfriend who happened to be at my home visiting on that day said, "Don't tell him anything yet! You have to do a blood test first." "I've already told him. He was excited. I also told him to standby because I knew that I had to do the blood test," I replied.

I worked at the hospital, so I went to my doctor and requested another pregnancy test. My doctor ordered a test for me. I was running late to a meeting and could not stay for the results. Luckily, my girlfriend was there, and she assured me that she would run the tests and notify me of the findings. Her notification could not come through fast enough. While sitting in the meeting, she sent me a message that read, "It was positive. Congratulations!" For me, time stood still in that moment. My heart had been set free. The moment that we stopped trying to get pregnant was when we conceived.

We establish a breeding ground for stress when we become so focused on what we desire. Sometimes, you just have to learn to trust in God. The Bible says to go forth and multiply. If our marriage was ordained and the Lord believed in multiplication, we must also believe that if his will is for us to have a family, it shall come to pass.

Although we were pregnant and ecstatic, we waited for three months before we told most of our family or friends. There was an extremely small group of family with whom we prematurely and cautiously shared our news. During the early part of the pregnancy, I was fine, and everything was going smoothly. Right around twenty-four weeks, I had my first major complication. I was sitting down when I felt a back-throbbing pain.

It hurt so badly. I forced myself to our bedroom and struggled with falling asleep, but I finally did. However, a throbbing pain woke me up very early in the morning because I could no longer take the pain. My brother, who happened to be visiting at the time was resting before his scheduled drive back home to Atlanta. I didn't want to wake him because I knew that he had a long drive ahead of him. The emergency room (ER) was right by my house, so I made the decision to walk there. I didn't trust myself to drive because of the immense pain. Upon my arrival, the ER staff thought I was insane for walking to the hospital in my current condition. They paged my doctor who showed up and was there for me. She checked, and said "You're not dilated, but I feel the baby's head." That was cause for concern. To gain more perspective, the doctor gave orders for the performance of an ultrasound. They determined that it wasn't the baby's head that was detected, it was a large fibroid. Coupled with the pregnancy, the fibroid had become inflamed. The doctor immediately ordered me to be placed on bed rest.

That was one of the hardest things I've ever done, because I'm used to waking up and being active. I was not a *bedrest* kind of lady. During that time, I tried to get a work computer, but my boss refused to accept my offer. "You're on bed rest, no work computer," she insisted. It was in that moment that I had to appreciate the act of sitting down and allowing my body to heal. Had I not been ordered to go on bedrest, I would have dragged myself to work each and every day. I had wanted this pregnancy so desperately, but I couldn't help but feel lonely as my husband was working in Europe, and I was in Mississippi, left to deal with the pain.

It was a trying period for me. I cried, and I was subliminally angry at my husband for not being there, but in my heart, I knew that he was doing the best he could for us. Your mind and your emotions are not always in sync. I knew in the back of my mind that he would have been with me if he could have. There were days that I couldn't walk. My brother, who had rearranged his schedule to help me, would carry me to the bathroom and to the couch. My sisters would come over and help as well as a few trusted friends. When I found out that I was pregnant, one of the nurses told me to not get excited until after nine weeks; in her words: "Most first pregnancies for young adult women end in miscarriage." Her words stuck with me and during those days when I was confined to the bed and the couch, I was constantly reminded that life was growing inside of me. For me, every day was a celebration. I knew that with every passing day, we were one day closer to meeting the baby that we had dreamed of. I recognized that every day that I was confined to that house was a day that my pregnancy would not end in miscarriage. I wanted nothing more than to welcome my baby into the world. I began to think of ways to keep my mind focused on positive aspects of life, and I was also in search of a way to share the truest emotions of my heart. I was in need of a mental escape. Journaling became my pastime of choice.

When I first started documenting my thoughts, I didn't know if I would have a girl or a boy. I just remember referring to the baby as "Angel". I would talk to her about the struggles I was going through, and I would write them in my journal. It felt so good to pour my heart out into words. Journaling quickly became my outlet. I talked to my husband multiple times a day and wrote often. My biggest struggle was that I didn't want to lose my baby. Many nights I cried and prayed. I didn't want to become the *sobby, pregnant lady*. I started working on using my journal as a tool for mental work. I began to do things that would keep me stimulated with very little physical activity. I started an online fitness shop, which kept me engaged. I had to undergo a mind shift; therefore, I began to realize that I shouldn't worry about things that I couldn't change. Increasingly, I came to realize the importance of shifting the energy that had once been categorized as worry to something productive.

My focus was now on being healthy, praying for my child, and finding ways to be constructive. The exercise of my mental strengths to do something more creative and help others became my fuel. In addition to journaling and the online shop, I did a lot of mentoring and coaching of women to discover their truths and purpose. These activities put me in a happy place. I was never the person who sat idle as time passed by. Taking control of my mental health and wealth, allowed me to channel joy deep on the inside. I got back to my happy place. The joy of my husband coming home, planning for baby showers, and believe me, I went big, and attending doctors appointments became what I looked forward to. There were days when the pain from the fibroids was too much to bear, but I knew better, and I allowed my body rest.

Discovering balance in that season was my greatest gift. We must never stop recentering ourselves and asking the question: Where should I focus my energy? There are times in our lives that our focus is unclear. We experience seasons that make us question what is important. The end goal should always be to do things that bring us joy in life. Journaling saved me in more ways than one. Committing my words to paper and honoring my feelings helped me to rediscover love. This love that I speak of is the limitless love that we all deserve. As women and as mothers, we are the cornerstone of love. Our ability to produce it is based on our ability to generate it within. It is my greatest hope that sharing my innermost thoughts on all things concerning motherhood with you, will serve as inspiration, motivation and strength to endure. The ability to think, to give, to thrive and to speak hope into the lives of others is a mother's greatest gift to the world. Giver of life, I have created this book with love for you.

Acknowledgments

I WOULD LIKE TO first give thanks to God who made everything possible.

To my husband: You are my love and life partner. Tse, thank you for being my cheerleader and believing in my vision and story. Thank you for your continuous support throughout this journey. I couldn't have achieved my dream of becoming a published author without you by my side.

Mummy and Papa: Thank you for instilling in me great values and for teaching me social responsibility. While some things didn't make sense growing up, I now understand them as an adult, and especially as a mother all too well. I remain appreciative and thankful to have you as my parents.

To my Siblings: Thank you for our inseparable bond. It is a blessing when you love the family you were born into, and they love you back equally. I didn't choose you, but our love is a testament to the fact that God's plan is perfect.

Adaora: You remind me that friendship is a gift that I must cherish. I thank God for you. Thank you for always being there and for always showing up.

Winifred: Your strength is beyond measure. You inspire me, and I'm thankful for your support and friendship.

Dr. Lacy: The world needs more doctors like you. Thank you for continuously making me feel safe and valued. Under your care, I trusted that my life and that of my growing babies were in good hands.

To my publisher: Ardre, the Queen of Storytelling, you are one phenomenal woman. Thank you for making this process seamless for me, and I look forward to all the greatness that's to come.

INTRODUCTION
AND AS A WOMAN THINKETH, SO SHALL SHE BE.

WHAT CAN BE said of motherhood? It is both challenging and rewarding, daunting and triumphant, disastrous and a series of unprecedented success. Motherhood is being all things to all people. And yet, there is no instructional manual that magically appears as we embark upon what evolves as a lifelong journey. There is so much to learn and so much to unpack that we are often left in search of answers.

The added responsibility of balancing work while nurturing lives and maintaining families add many more layers to what we are expected to be and do in this role. While we aim to please, the most important persons that we must garner a sense of satisfaction from, when it is all said and done, is ourselves. The only way to conceive the magnitude of strength that is required in this role is to access an internal breeding ground for positivity. This pool of reinforcement can only be cultivated amidst a positive mindset. Waiting for others to foster an environment from which to thrive is not effective. We must be the source of inspiration for ourselves and others.

Although challenging, we were divinely appointed to impart the substance of all things hoped for in the world. Our hearts are the gardens of love from which all good and perfect things grow.

ONLY A POSITIVE mindset will allow us to be the well that houses the water that our loved ones and the world needs. Motherhood in the truest form resembles harmony. Taking the lead to create an environment that is both fulfilling and harmonious can have lasting effects on the byproducts that we present to the world. It is important that we maintain a cache of strategies to remain positive when the going gets tough to relieve our minds from stress factors of which we are not always aware. The right mindset dictates that you only take the important things seriously. There is too little time to concern ourselves with factors that will not matter in the long run. Our energy must be directed towards what we believe to be most important for the overall health and sustainability of our families and ourselves, which is the key to balance.

Simply stated, there are times when we worry about things that don't matter. We must learn to focus on the end goal. We must ask ourselves why we feel the way that we do and directly address our emotional needs in response to what is important. We must learn to relinquish the burden of undue stress. We don't take full advantage of the precious time that has been gifted to us when we concern ourselves with miniscule factors.

RELEASE THE STRESS. IT IS NOT YOURS.

WE IMPEDE PROGRESS for all when we allow ourselves to be distracted by the opinions of others regarding our parenting. Attempts to control others and the challenges as opposed to the solutions that arise in our daily lives can lead to misuse of time. Recognizing the value of the people in your life is the ultimate definition of love. Empowering yourself to see life from a variety of perspectives is love. Recognizing that there is not one way to do life or parenting is love.

CHANGE YOUR PERSPECTIVE.

PERSPECTIVE IS EVERYTHING. The window from which we view the world determines what we can achieve and what we perceive as our capabilities. It is imperative that we perceive from a position of power. What we believe and our scope of ability are transferred to our children. If we deem ourselves capable, our children will deem themselves capable. We are their first teachers and the cultivators of their perspective. It is so easy to think about the worst in every situation before you begin to think about the good. What if we spent more time assuming that people's intentions were good? What if we restored faith in ourselves before allowing the spirit of doubt to set in? We must work to consider how changing the narrative can change our lives for the better. What can you do to see the positivity in the world?

The right mindset permits us to go about our days, not worrying about insignificant things. We become more in sync with our purpose as mothers and wives when we focus our hearts and our attention on the things and people that matter. This perspective is the key to adding value to our lives on a daily basis. A shift in perspective can turn a negative into a positive. The way in which we treat ourselves, conduct business, and run our households shifts should be channeled through positive energy at all times. We must challenge ourselves to accept nothing less. Learning to entrust that our lives will fall into divine order and working to shift our thinking toward the situations and solutions as opposed to the people who create them is key. We are certain to reap a harvest when our thoughts are pure and planted in the realm of possibilities. As a mother, anything is possible. The greatest fruit that we can bear is a productive citizen, refined, ready, willing and able to make the world a better place.

The pages of this book are filled with the greatest sentiments of my heart and all of the invaluable lessons that I wish someone had shared with me before embarking upon the journey of motherhood. The real truth is that motherhood is not the same for everyone. We will all experience life through our respective lenses.

It is my belief that the most powerful act that we can engage in is to share our experiences in an unfiltered, transparent way, as we find ourselves fighting for balance, managing expectations, and channeling love. Memoirs of A Working Mother is my greatest gift to you. Read with your whole heart.

Table of Contents

I: FIGHTING FOR BALANCE

1: The Wait...41
2: Communicating Effectively......................53
3: Getting Tasks Done and Leveraging
   Organization..69
4: Single Wives and Single Mothers.............81
5: Sleeping and Resting..............................89
6: Self-Talk and Affirmative Actions..............95
CONCLUSIVE THOUGHT: Discover Happiness.....99
CAVEAT: From the Outside In........................101

II: MANAGING EXPECTATIONS

7. Construct A House or Build A Home?.......109
8: Finances...115
9: Expectations in the Workplace................119
10: Time Management...............................127

11: Motherhood and Being in Business 135
12: Things No One Ever Told You 147
13: Mind Over Matter 155

III: CHANNELING LOVE

14: Self-Love 165
15: Mental Health 173
16: Postpartum Depression 189
17: Breastfeeding 195
18: Fibroids 207
19: The Silent Fear 219
20: The Law of Attraction 223
CONCLUSIVE THOUGHT: A Four Letter Word ... 227
CAVEAT: Be the Light 229
IV. Epilogue: The Joys of Motherhood 231
V. Dear Working Mother 233
VI. Executing Your Goals 239
VII. Take the
#21DAYWORKINGMOTHER
Challenge 243
MEET AND CONNECT with Linda Arrey 267

I.
FIGHTING FOR BALANCE

"The only way to maintain your balance is to keep moving."
-Linda Arrey-

[HOW DO YOU DEFINE BALANCE?]

DEFINE BALANCE BY acknowledging the fact that it does not always exist. Most people think about perfection when referencing the concept of balance. In life and in motherhood, balance is not synonymous with suddenly attaining a constant level of stability. Stability is seasonal in our lives. A lot of people think that a working/life balance means that you have everything under control all the time. Disappointment can arise when you have high expectations for yourself, and you don't meet those expectations, especially when time is a concern. You can feel as though you have fallen short.

The word balance implies a steady position so that things do not falter. Stability is necessary so that you don't fail, but it doesn't denote a constant state of equilibrium in life. Serving as a mother alters the equilibrium when you have a schedule, and things will not always go according to plan. Many factors affect our day to day activity; therefore, balance becomes a constant strive for a state of equilibrium. You must take comfort in knowing that you are striving for it, even on days when you don't attain it. Walking around with a fulfilled mindset allows you to be more productive because you recognize the possibilities. A sense of fulfillment enhances your desire to wake up every day and to keep going. Creating a work life balance is owning the fact that balance is a journey, not a destination.

[WHAT DOES SOCIETY TELL WOMEN AND MOTHERS ABOUT BALANCE?]

WE LIVE IN a society where women constantly have to prove themselves. We have to prove ourselves at home and prove ourselves in board rooms. People assume that we won't perform at our best because we are women. There are people who do not respect women in leadership positions, until there is demonstration of certain milestones. As a woman, you have to prove yourself repeatedly. Even if you have the title and the qualifications, you have to go in there and prove yourself. Respect is earned for us, not given because we have attained a certain level of success or achieved a specific goal. Society generalizes that women are incompetent, and there is a tendency to look for failure. To the contrary, women are taught to perform at a high level because so much is expected of us. We are asked and are expected to do a great deal of work in every setting.

The good news is that we have the power to influence our environments and to change the culture to value everyone who contributes. We have the power to bring about a positive perception of our actions and thoughts. Sometimes, we just have to block out the noise. People can only judge so much, but if you listen and you give into their draining dispositions, they can influence you. Block out the noise and prove yourself based upon your own set of rules. We don't have to remain fixated on the bias that we all know exist. We can, instead, be the solution that we know is so desperately needed by all women who fall victim to societally imposed imbalance. We live in a biased society. If a man walks into a room, he is immediately respected. We combat many ill intents in the workplace, and they affect our ability to balance all that is thrown our way.

I don't want women to be shy or timid about their abilities. I want women to know their self-worth. If a woman walks into an environment and she feels disrespected or someone attempts to make her feel less than, I want her to have the qualifications and the skills to silence the noise.

In the home, expectations can vary. Every home is different and the rules that govern the attitudes and climate are specific to that home. The expectations in your home depend on your spouse. Do you have someone who is supportive, or do you have someone who believes that he is doing you a favor? Does your partner think that he should babysit his child? Do you have someone who will assist you if he has had a shorter day at work? Are you married to someone who would advise you to put your feet up while he makes dinner? The man is to be respected as the head of the house, and this is not a bad thing. Men serving as leaders should not negate the fact that they too can assist and work as a member of the team to accomplish the daily goals in the home.

As women, we have been gifted with the ability to manage tasks as they are completed. We are naturally gifted with managerial skills. Our proficiency is demonstrated as we manage finances and operations while being great mothers who nurture and care for their children. I believe that we must disregard much of what society dictates in order to establish our own roles in our homes. This is my idea of creating balance in the home. We know how we can better take care of the family and ourselves, and all of the notions that society recommends must be viewed as examples. There are many men who are excellent cooks, child care providers and homemakers. The more we establish the rules and roles for our homes, the more we access the fruits of our labor and expose ourselves and our families to the concept of balance.

[WHO TEACHES US WHAT ROLES EACH PARENT PLAYS IN YOUR HOME?]

I GREW UP watching my mom and dad (Mummy and Papa, as I call them), in their roles as parents and husband and wife. I came from a traditional African family, and there were many practices and customs that were staples. God was always first. My dad was the spiritual leader of our home. My mother was his helpmate and my dad's better half. We, the children were the fruits of their harvest. African men believe that they are financially responsible for the home. My father felt that it was his responsibility to make sure that the children were fed and had a roof over their heads. However, my mother also worked. She was a teacher. The times that she said she wanted to go back to school, Dad encouraged her to do so. My mom would cook and inform my father of our needs. My father would strategize financially and oversee how the money was spent.

We were taught by example that it is okay for the wife to submit to the husband. It made sense as men were the heads of the home.

[HOW DOES A BALANCED HOME SERVE AS A PRECURSOR FOR A FAMILY'S SUCCESS?]

WHEN YOU HAVE balance at home, you're more productive in other areas of your life. You are more aware of what is expected of you, and your spouse is more aware of what is expected of him. Emotionally, there are grounds for sustainability because you feel a sense of fulfillment. This can not ring true in instances where one spouse does not do their part. Marriage and family is a team effort, no matter how traditional someone is in their values or their perspectives on the roles that each spouse plays. If your position is that of a deadbeat at home, respect and trust can easily be lost. Respect and trust are two of the attributes that glue families together in love. As a woman, it is imperative that we know what we want and the level of efficiency in which we want our homes to run. There are times that we have too many expectations for others. We must discover the balance in how we hold ourselves and others accountable. Learning to be realistic is critical. When you operate within the guidelines of realistic expectations and your goals are rooted in nurturing the needs of everyone, including yourself, you will watch your children thrive and the invaluable smile on your husband's face.

ONE

THE WAIT

"Consider giving up who you once were to become the woman you've always had the potential to become."
-Linda Arrey-

AS I APPROACHED my late twenties, many people began to express their growing concerns for my singleness. For some reason, society makes us feel that we are deeply troubled and damaged goods if we are not married by the age of thirty. I was getting phone calls from guys who told me that my aunt had given them my number. It was as if I had reached a point of desperation. I had to go as far as putting my entire family on notice that I did not grant permission for my phone number to be randomly distributed to potential suitors. I'd say "Please do not give my number out." Things reached a tipping point when I discovered that my family was dispersing my number as freely as business cards to potential single men that they would come in contact with. My aunts would exclaim: "Oh, you're single. Let me give you my niece's number."

I even met guys who would say "Ugh! you're pretty, and you're so successful, why aren't you married?" It seemed as though the only reliable explanation for me not being married was that something was gravely wrong with me. No one seemed to have realized that I had developed a low tolerance for foolishness from men. If you pay close attention, you can recognize when someone is not worth your time. The older you get, the less time you wish to waste. I could tell in a few minutes if I would actually be calling or losing a guy's number. When I met my husband, it all felt right. I'm not saying that I walked into a fairytale or that I was shot by Cupid, it was more special than that. I listened to him when he talked, and it was like "Thank you, Jesus". There were subtle factors that made me take special note of who he was. He was the missing piece of the puzzle.

By the time I met my husband, I was at a place where I was ready to get married. Not only was I ready to enter into a union with someone, but I also felt as though I was ready to start a family. It had been almost three years since the last time I actually dated. I was in my *waiting* period. I reference this period as a time of waiting because it denotes that you are taking time to discover yourself. Dating can complicate things and cloud your judgement. If you don't take careful observation to truly understand what you want from yourself, it becomes increasingly difficult to place such demands on others. During my wait, I was connecting spiritually, getting right with God, and getting to a place where I felt fulfillment within myself. I believe that we must learn to be happy alone before we can ever realize happiness with someone else. Not only was I happy with my personal life, I was also content with my professional life. These factors were clues that I was ready to build a relationship with someone else.

I was not looking for someone to complete me; I was in search of someone with whom I could share with in the building process. I was in search of someone who could bring an added level of energy that would empower us to coexist and construct a life together. With this mindset, I knew that I desired a partnership with someone that I could walk hand in hand with through life.

INTENTIONALITY

I KNOW THAT I am not the only person who has heard men say "It seems like every woman wants to get married." What's wrong with that? Women should be able to communicate their intentions up front. There is a stigma that women should shy away from the conversation and allow men to figure it out. What if the man that you are dating does not want to be married to you? Why waste valuable time that could be spent bettering yourself or with a person who is interested in a relationship that results in marriage? I don't advise that we shy away from expressing what we desire in a relationship.

On one occasion, my cousin called me to chat. As the conversation continued, she expressed that she wanted to be married. My response was "then why are you casually dating?"

There is nothing wrong with casual dating, but it is my belief that purposeful dating yields can be more meaningful. I further explained that if a woman desires a lasting relationship, then that information should be shared up front. On the contrary, if she was only dating for companionship, then she should carry on. I am a believer in courtship.

The bottom line is that life is too short and the opportunity for love does not knock at your door every day. I also don't believe that we should waste time when we've found the right one.

When I met my husband, I knew that he was special.

Never in a million years would I have guessed that a chance meeting on a bus would lead to a lifetime of happiness together. The bus had broken down, forcing all of the passengers to exit. As we stood around, taking advantage of the food vendors, while waiting to be informed of what would happen next, he approached me. Engaged in light-hearted conversation, he looked straight into my eyes and said: "You are going to be my wife." I chuckled and didn't take him seriously. However, he was determined, yet kind and gentle when he spoke. He asked me for my contact information. I was intrigued and I obliged.

From that day forward, we remained connected. He would always refer to me as his wife in his emails. After dating for a short period of time, he would return to Europe. We would discover it to be increasingly hard to maintain a long distance relationship at the time.

In retrospect, I can deduce that we were both young and I was very much learning to recognize what I truly desired in a lifetime partner. I was twenty-one, and he was twenty-four at the time. In the absence of our long-distance connection, I continued to discover myself and to listen to the voice inside that would eventually guide my internal messaging about love and the life I desired.

In a period of ten years, I evolved personally and professionally. I fell in love with myself. Although I knew that I one day wanted to be married, I was content with who I had become and the way in which I valued myself. And then one day, true love discovered me. I received a random message on Facebook but I didn't quite recognize who it was from. The profile had no specific photo. I began to look on the person's page in hopes of identifying who it was, and my discovery brought me much excitement. It was Tse.

We found ourselves reconnecting at a period in my life where I was now very clear on what I wanted for my future and the person that I would be blessed to share it with. I didn't hold back. I was open and honest and shared my deepest sentiments and desires with him.

Our communication and exchanges felt right. For that reason alone, I needed to let him know that I was not interested in dating casually. I was open for courtship and a serious commitment. I shared with him that I was not looking to be fulfilled because I had discovered how to do that for myself. I wanted him to know without question that I was looking for what it appeared that we could have together. I shared so transparently with him because in just a few days he made me believe that he was the one, and it felt right. I can remember that when I told him exactly what I wanted, at first, he was quiet on the phone, but eventually, he started talking and sharing more. He later shared with me that he was not shocked, he was just not used to people expressing their feelings so candidly. We recognized that we both shared in the desire to commit. We were in each other's presence for the prospect of a future together. Upon our third conversation, he asked me to marry him. Our dating was the evolution of an open and honest courtship. Six months later, we were married.

CULTURE AND THE CULTIVATION OF A UNION

COMING FROM AN African family, it's important for our families to bless our marriages. Prior to my husband and I getting married, our families had disagreements about our union. By the time we made the decision to get married, I was thirty, and he was thirty-four. We were waiting patiently for their blessing. It meant so much to us to have them support our union. We had garnered the support of our siblings. They had demonstrated their approval, but not our parents. We paused to consider if we were doing the wrong thing? I began to question myself. Had we been mistaken in deciding to choose one another? I started to pray and fast in hopes of God sending me answers. The day before I broke my fast, I was convinced that we were right for each other. Around midnight, I called my father, and

I told him that I felt in my heart that I had chosen the man for me. I asked my father for his blessing. I wanted my father to know that his approval was vital to me. That night, my father told me that he would open his heart to think about it. My father said to me that he would need three days to consider his feelings and thoughts on the matter. I was filled with unspeakable joy when I learned that my father was on board with the wedding. Everybody on both sides came around and the few who didn't, well we can only continue to show them our love each day.

We still have some aunts and uncles who are upset to this day that we got married without asking for their permission. In my culture, relatives feel entitled to give their input about the decisions that you make about your life. From my perspective, our parents were on board, so it was the permission we needed to move forward. At the time of our union, my husband was living overseas, and I was in the US. There were times that he would come home for three days then be gone for months. On other occasions, he would come back for two weeks and then be gone for five months. We wanted a family but also questioned if we would have the capacity to do so as he was not home the majority of the time.

We were not just at the mercy of our parents for approval of our marriage, but we also discovered that we would stand in need of the grace of the Chief Magistrate.

Upon our arrival at the courthouse, things appeared to be out of sync. The judge that was to oversee the process was not present. We found this as a surprise as we had set our appointment accordingly. We would have assumed that something of this magnitude would not result in a missed appointment.

We were given a list of locations that we could go to complete the process.

Disheveled, we began to search for a name on the list to find someone that could be of assistance to us.

After selecting a judge, we left the courthouse to report to the address provided.

Upon our arrival, we were introduced to Chief Magistrate Dallas, who happened to be a woman. We had no idea what to expect and then she began to speak, yielding her thoughts on marrying us. "I have to make sure it's right in my heart and that this union is ordained." We were taken aback in many ways. Even though she was the Chief Magistrate, she was still biblical. In a position such as hers, it was refreshing to see someone put spirituality first and to use it as the foundation of commitment. She spoke to our hearts and ministered to our families.

She was insightful and charismatic and her wisdom proved to be priceless beyond measure. She gave me a very poignant perspective on being a strong woman in a relationship and gave me perspective on my husband's disposition in our lives. "Madame CEO, you are a powerful woman. You must learn to shift to the side and let a man lead. You've spent so many years taking care of others, but he's a first-born son who has been taking care of siblings. He knows how to lead." She recognized specific characteristics and the details of our personalities. The entire experience was surreal. It felt like she had known us for years. She even went off script, and dived into ministering into our lives during the ceremony. We entrusted that moment and the bond that would live on forever to her wisdom on that day.

We knew with certainty that our journey was ordained because of circumstances surrounding how we found ourselves in her office, and the powerful way in which she ministered to us. We will always be thankful that she was sent to orchestrate our union.

Her presence and her actions were another confirmation to us that God had ordered our steps. We knew that we would be blessed if we resolved to keep our love first.

TWO
COMMUNICATING EFFECTIVELY

"My heart speaks with love."
-Linda Arrey -

EPHESIANS 5:22-32

YOUR MARRIAGE IS your ministry. When we treat our union like a ministry, it's easier for us to communicate effectively as our thoughts are deeply rooted in love.

We are well informed as to the roles of the husband, wife, and children, according to the Bible. It teaches us a great deal about our disposition in the family. Often, the lines of communication regarding those roles are blurred because people are getting into marriages for the title, versus doing the work to build a solid foundation for their families. Society has communicated to us that marriage is an accomplishment. In the Biblical sense, many refer to the Proverbs version of what a woman is to be. Society dictates that women are to cook, clean, and take care of the home. I argue that the same Bible talks about the role of the man. How often does society broadcast the role of the man in the marriage? We must acquaint ourselves with the concept of the triangle in our relationships. The marriage relationship is a triangle. It's a relationship between God, man, and wife. When you put God at the center of the marriage, all energy flows from God to the husband and then to the wife. If any part of the triangle is broken, the other end cannot honor its part of the relationship. It's a continuous process and one that evolves. We must reverence this concept in our quest to effectively communicate our needs, and desires in our marriages.

SOCIETY AND SUBMISSION

SUBMISSIVENESS HAS BECOME a trending topic. The Bible dictates that wives should submit to their husbands. How often do we refer to scripture found in Ephesians that dictates that husbands should love their wives just as Jesus loved the church? The same Bible that urges wives to submit also encourages husbands to give themselves up for their wives. If a husband can have that insurmountable kind of love for his wife, then he possesses the ability to treat her with honor and respect because he is treating her as he would treat himself. A husband would give himself up for his wife because he would save his own life. In today's society, we are so profoundly focused on the roles of the wife and the term submissiveness, and we miss the bigger picture. We are so fixated on the cooking and cleaning and managing of the home that we fail to acknowledge that the wife is also called to be in a relationship that is filling her cup as she gives of herself. The Bible teaches us that the wife should also benefit from the marriage, just as those that she is cooking, cleaning and caring for would. A deeper understanding helps us to recognize the giving and taking that compose a marriage. These factors, alone, demand effective communication to reap the benefits of all the prosperity that the union can yield.

Many women get into a marriage and conform to the societal imposed norms of their role without ever truly knowing their husband's expectations. It's important to first understand what your husband believes you are responsible for in the home. What actions does he consider himself to be accountable for executing? If you know where you stand and what your role is, it is much easier to identify when specific needs are not being met on either side. When a marriage is built on Biblical principles, it is easy to recognize when your needs are not being met, and you can recognize what you bring to the table and how you should be treated; therefore, it is easier to engage in an honest exchange about the voids that you can potentially feel. If you are in tune with what you want and how you desire to be treated, you can easily recognize what you want as well as what you are missing.

Many women don't know how they should be treated. When society says that you should be submissive to your husband and that you don't deny him when he wants sex, you feel as if you are not honoring your role if you compromise or challenge these standards. The more significant question is: what works for your marriage? If you've been up since 4:30 am getting the kids ready for school, and pumping milk for the baby, and you are responsible for dropping the kids off at school and going to work, it is highly possible that you are exhausted. When you return home to settle the children, clean and make dinner, only to clean again, do you have the right to say that you are too tired for sex? If the Bible advises you to submit to your husband, and that is your only interpretation, is it possible that the answer is *no*? However, if your husband loves you in the same way that Christ loves the church, then he would be more understanding. He would wake up with you, and at times, offer to extend your sleep. Maybe your husband can offer to get a bottle ready for the baby in order to give you a few additional moments to gather yourself. A loving husband is the ultimate team player. The only way to attain family goals of this magnitude is effective communication. There is no way to predict what your spouse is thinking, nor should you try. Finding ways to express how you can best support each other is critical. Moreover, while society would lead us to believe that one party has to suffer and that everyone's needs can't possibly be met are notions that are far from the truth. When communication happens effectively, happiness can be discovered by all.

SPEAK WITH YOUR HEART

AS MOTHERS, WE often proclaim how tired we are and wonder why no one seems to understand. The hard truth is that simply proclaiming "I'm tired" without saying why you are tired is not good enough to elicit empathy from those that we love. We would love to believe that anyone who bears witness to the many tasks that we manage in a day would not need an explanation. Stopping to consider that those whom we serve are focused on their own needs, and this alleviates your anxiety of not being understood. In professing to the world that you are tired, you are not communicating where you need help or what you see as shortcomings. In order to communicate effectively, you have to know your role and your husband's role. You need to be able to clearly state how others can assist you. Have you considered what you need help with? Have you asked for help? It is very possible that those around you are helping in the ways that they know. This does not, however, mean that it is help in the way that you want it. As mothers, we become fixated on having things done a certain way, sometimes to a fault. If the only way that things can be done is the way that meets our expectations, then we must also be okay with not receiving help from others. Something as simple as setting a designated time for your kids to go to bed to have quality time with your spouse or a moment for yourself can make all the difference in the world. Why do we so often assume that no one wants to help us?

Mothers can always benefit from having additional helping hands. When I feel I need help, I know that I can count on my husband, he is always there to lend a helping hand as I am for him.

In moments when I get upset about things that he is completely unaware of, as women sometimes do, I've been known to give a little of the silent treatment here and there. It never works. By the time I express my feelings, he is often appalled. He wouldn't have sensed that I was ever even upset, because it had not occurred to him. Why is it that we want our husbands to read our minds? I've since learned that if only I had spoken to him in love to express my feelings, he would have done all that he could have to meet my needs.

I've also taken time to identify moments that are conducive for conversations of the heart. After dinner, when everyone is calm, we sit together and truly indulge in good conversation. We have managed to create a safe zone for open and honest exchanges. During those moments, I can relax and talk about the stress at work and anything else that may be going on. Afterwards, I am always surprised at how much better I feel. There are times when I recognize that the misplaced stress was never about someone washing the dishes or wiping down the table. On so many occasions, a listening ear was all the therapy I needed. In those moments when I resolve to pull my hair out because of something insignificant, I am reminded that I really just need him to sit and listen. I've also made it a point to reinforce him by showing appreciation for his presence. Effective communication executed in the home also means expressing gratitude for those that we love. My approach with my husband has also evolved over time. I begin each day in consideration of what I can do to make his day brighter. I've adopted the perspective that communication in a marriage is not about what my husband can do for me. Effective communication is about what we can do for each other. As humans, it is in our nature to be selfish and put our needs first in relationships. However, it is my belief that the more effort we exert towards making each other happy, the more positive energy we will circulate in our home.

GENDER. LEADERSHIP. MATRIMONY.

AS THE DISCUSSION of gender related issues ensues, we must acknowledge that there is a stigma attached to being a woman. Society leads us to believe that women always fight to be right. I don't believe this to be the case as much as I think that we must consider the passion behind what women fight for. We are wired to discover the inequalities and injustices. Our nature commands that we even the playing field for everyone, including ourselves. I like it when my husband gives me his opinion versus just agreeing with me. It is my belief that women enjoy seeing issues from a variety of perspectives. I need a man that can tell me that I'm wrong so that I can grow. We should marry strong men that can lead us spiritually and in our quest to develop both personally and professionally. Men who are respectful inspire women to honor and respect them in their capacities as leaders. When we marry men that we can't respect, they don't meet the qualifications to lead. We live in a society where respect is assigned by virtue of actions. As women, we have to work twice as hard to earn the respect of our peers and among staff in professional settings. Thus, it should come as no surprise that we will only follow men who garner our respect in our homes.

In the workplace, a lot of people respect the title but not the person sitting in the office. This can lead to disputes and a lack of authority. The home is no different. If a woman focuses on getting married for the title, with little to no emphasis on respect for the husband's role, problems are sure to arise. I'd even venture to say that it is wrong to marry just for the sake of bearing the title "wife". It is imperative that we marry someone that we would willingly submit ourselves to.

I can speak for most women when I say that we want and need a man that we feel comfortable relying on in good times and bad. We need men that we can cultivate a relationship with that evolves over time. We want our husbands to be in the position of honor and respect. If a woman truly wants the best for her family, she will not desire to have a lack of respect for her husband. In this same frame of reference, no one wants to work for a boss that they don't respect in the workplace. Based on all that we are called to do, we instinctively respect those who possess an ability to make sound decisions and those who demonstrate solid skills from which to lead. When we effectively discuss and understand our roles in both the home and workplaces, we create a clear perspective to govern ourselves accordingly.

THE CHAIN OF COMMAND

IN THE WORKPLACE, the roles and responsibilities are easily deciphered. Whether there is an organizational chart that is adhered to or you have been verbally instructed on what is expected of you and others, the lines are seldom grey. When you become a wife and a mother, the lines can become blurred, because our biological instincts lead us to put our children first. It is possible that because we carry children in our wombs, we feel more responsible for their well being. This is not, however, what God intended. We are not able to produce children alone, nor are we responsible for caring for them on our own. In my home, I take careful consideration to put my husband first. Our home dictates that it is he and I against the world. I love my husband and children equally, but my husband will always come first. We lead our children according to God's will. It is important to me that our children recognize that my husband is first. We are the parents, and they are to respect our position to lead them effectively. In my home, the chain of command is: God, the husband, the wife, and the children. I have even worked diligently to replace the notion of a mother child relationship with a parental relationship. Children can benefit so greatly from being nurtured by both mother and father. All things considered, I realize that there are attributes and qualities that we can both give to our children that are unique to each of us. The key is in remembering that every player in the game is important. We need each other to achieve the life that we have dreamed of together. Placing emphasis on raising our children together, teaches them to recognize the importance of working together and imparting vision for the family. As mothers and wives, the way in which we communicate is not about being the boss, it is about taking ownership of and pride in the ministry that we have been blessed to oversee.

OWNING YOUR *NO*

WHEN I HAD my first born child, my husband was in Europe. I was a single wife and the responsibility continued to increase. My saving grace was learning to say "no" in exchange for time with my family. What could be more valuable? And as much as I wanted to perform above and beyond every time at my job, I simply could not. I still put in my one hundred percent. I remember sitting in a meeting where we were asked to discuss any challenges we were facing on or off the job, and how our leadership could better assist us with executing our respective roles. I asked for flexibility, and further explained some challenges I was experiencing parenting our daughter alone with my husband in another continent. To my surprise, another colleague, someone I also considered a friend, said: "I get what you are saying, but to be fair, the military doesn't pay us all this money so we can have children." I was baffled at her limiting mindset. My thought process was the extreme opposite. I felt as though the military wasn't paying me all of that money to stop living. Starting a family is part of living. The colleague who made this statement was single and didn't have children of her own yet, so I could understand why she didn't understand my perspective. Not only had I learned to say "no" to constraints imposed by my job that forced me to neglect my responsibilities of motherhood, but I had also learned to reject the thoughts and sentiments of others that did not align with my vision for myself personally and professionally. We must learn to ground our decision making in the value that we possess and our contributions to each entity that we are a part of.

I refused to allow my uniform or the opinions of others to impede me from becoming a mother. When we allow others to dictate the guidelines that we set for ourselves based on their beliefs and opinions, it might be harmful to the construct of our families. This is not the definition of balance. We approach life through our own respective lenses. We have had different childhood and life experiences that shape and mold our ideals of what we will create for ourselves. All things considered, it is not always sound advice that we receive from others. I can remember some of the people that I worked with were angry that I came into work a little later on the occasions that I had to change my daughter again before leaving the house. As a mother, the notion of anyone having anything negative to say about a mother caring for her child was something that I did not agree with. To those professionals with whom I worked, who did not place value on creating families of their own, my disposition was unrealistic. I rejected their perspectives as they did not align with mine. I knew that I had the power to take care of my daughter, be present at the meeting and yield results worthy of validation at work.

Although I am still very much dedicated to excellence in my career, I've found some success along the way. I have won some higher level rewards and experienced some recognition, while being a mother. I've managed to accomplish so much, while being a mother. I've learned to decipher the difference between not performing and performing differently or more efficiently to meet the needs of several different demands. Like anyone else, I've had days when I questioned if I could do it all, or if I were capable, but I pushed harder, and I succeeded.

I balanced it all because I set goals and boundaries. Had I allowed others to limit my potential, I would have never known my capabilities and how much I could balance personally and professionally.

I don't want any working mother to be employed at a place that does not value her. We shouldn't be forced to compromise going to work every day and doing what we love for being the best parents that we can be.

THREE

GETTING TASKS DONE AND LEVERAGING ORGANIZATION

"Organization is a rare form of empowerment."
-Linda Arrey-

WHEN YOU START having children, you don't want to mitigate your duties, but you do have to reconsider your strategy to get it all done. With an emphasis on caring for new life, you don't have to overcompensate in the same ways that you did before becoming a mother. There are times when we burden ourselves with guilt for not being the same person that we were before embarking upon the lifelong journey of motherhood. Everything will change after the arrival of an addition to the family, and rightfully so. As a mother, your time has to be allocated differently. As much as we would like to believe that life will be intact after the arrival of the baby, it will not. The reality of change can be a rude awakening for those who fight to keep everything the same. New and seasoned mothers benefit from embracing the element of transition. As our babies grow, the cycles of our lives and the dynamics of our families evolve. We never return to the same dimensions as family life forces us to stretch and grow. When embraced, growth is a beautiful thing.

RETURNING TO THE WORKFORCE

YOU CAN'T REALISTICALLY go back to work after having a baby and exert the same energy, because you are now responsible for directing a great deal of that energy towards caring for your family. Your time is divided and your responsibilities have changed; however, you still have the same twenty-four hour period to balance it all. It's okay to change the parameters of what you can offer. There is no harm in evolution. Being realistic and transparent about what you know you can accomplish is crucial for a mother who is balancing a return to work. We must be careful not to overpromise and under deliver. The goal must be to discover your threshold for the completion of tasks and the execution of family goals. Break down your twenty-four hours and allocate time towards what you deem priority. Whether it's eight hours to sleep, two hours of *you time*, nine hours of work, and four hours of family time, every hour matters. Daily family time should not be optional.

You will perform differently after becoming a mother, but this does not denote that your performance is not just as effective as it has been prior to giving birth. You can still close those deals, but you might need to get creative to establish a different formula. Every new mother needs to redefine herself and learn to reallocate her time. Maybe it's time to be more cautious of what you accept on your plate. When it was just you, you could take on every assignment thrown your was, but now you have to make sure you're not neglecting yourself, your children, and your husband.

When at work, there are times that you must make the decision to go home. Spending time with family, making dinner, and setting aside time for yourself prove to be just as important as performing in excellence at your place of work. While at work, you want to ask yourself if it can wait until tomorrow, especially if you are working during some of the hours that you could be at home with your children and spouse. Dedicating time to your family is paramount. I have always believed that family and time spent engaged with family are important, but this tradition has continued to ring true through the years. When we cultivate our families and work to ensure that our structure is built upon a solid foundation, we reap a harvest that we cannot gather from work alone. Work is meant to sustain us financially, and we are called to do our jobs with care and to take pride in attaining success. As a mother, understanding the importance of family helps us to take this concept to heart.

It is so important that we become wise through our experiences and that we acquire wisdom by seeking it from those who have lived the lives that we aspire to. I was given some very sound advice, during a lunch with a General. I asked the question: "Sir, as a General, what life lessons have you used to govern you through a successful career?" The reply was profound. "Work is never too important. You have to find a way to attend those dance recitals and school games. At the end of the day, when I retire this uniform, my family is all I have." It was in that moment that I realized that you don't have to be in the military to have that mindset. A working mother from any profession will want to be able to retire and have time to watch the fruits of her labor as her family flourishes. In society, we are cultivated to not prioritize family in many ways. We are putting so much pressure on ourselves to acquire money for material things for our families. While the desire to take care of our families with essentials like food to eat, a home to live in and a car to drive makes perfect sense, why do we sacrifice quality time for the extras that are not necessities? We become so invested in the process of acquiring the money, but we miss the process of sewing into the livelihood of our families.

We must take the time to discover a formula that allows us to reach our goals in the personal and professional arenas of our lives while determining what is going to work for us. When creating your strategy for balance, keep in mind that it does not need to mirror anyone else's strategy. Your balance might not reflect that of the mother down the street who works and cares for her family. Your balance might look completely different from the mother who decides to remain at home with her children. All balance is not created equally, and that's acceptable. It's all about working collaboratively with your husband or support system to determine how to serve as a pillar for your family. The goal must always be to establish a lasting legacy with your family that will positively impact generations to come.

Each week I have a list of things to accomplish, and this list helps to keep me on track. The question must always be--how can you make your time more valuable? It's not quantity but the quality of what you are producing that matters most. You have to maximize your time. Although I don't recommend it for everyone, I engage in a working lunch on most days. I reallocated that time for the completion of minor tasks. I also don't hesitate to take a mental break when I need it. If sacrificing those thirty minutes to an hour can put me back at home with my family faster, that will always be my choice. You have to look at your circumstances and decide where you can spend more time. Some days I am late for work because I need extra time to get out of the house with the children. Some days my daughter will have the biggest "poop" right when I'm about to leave the house. I'm not going to drive sixteen miles with her unclean and suffer through a "poop" infused ride to work and school. I will stop and change her. The logistics of the job can evolve and force you to reallocate your time. In my place of work, I have a different boss every two years, so it is possible that the dynamics will change. Every person has a different leadership style and adjustments must be made. I communicate with my leadership team, so I know what they expect. I make sure that my work is consistent and completed with quality.

One major aspect of delivering quality work is the professionals with whom we choose to surround ourselves. It is also important, whenever possible, to have a supportive staff. Although we don't always get to choose who is by our side in the workplace, we must find ways to establish meaningful relationships. It is crucial to find an accountability partner, who has your best interest in mind. If I'm putting in long days, my accountability partner will call me out. If you effectively communicate what you want to attain both personally and professionally, this person can assist you in maintaining balance. This is my balance, and I need you to call me out when I'm swaying from that. When we get so focused on specific areas or the completion of certain tasks, we can get turned around to discover that we are fully immersed. We need someone to remind us of the balance that we were once determined to discover.

There are times when the discoverance of a sound mind prove to be the most powerful for me. I like to tap into inspiration. Along my drive to work, I will often play music that inspires me to engage in praise and worship. On other days, I drive in silence and meditate amidst my thoughts. My motto is to make every minute count.

When changes occur and disrupt the stability of the equilibrium, you have to find a new way to balance. Life and all that we are responsible for gets easier, when we learn to manage all that is thrown our way.

CHOOSING THE RIGHT DAYCARE

DROPPING OFF MY babies for the first time at daycare remains one of the hardest things I have done as a mother. Some Days, it was harder for me than is was for our girls. "Will they be okay? Will they be properly taken care of? Will they be comforted when they cry? Will their diapers be changed in a timely fashion?" These are questions that clouded my mind. I cried on most days. As time progressed and I saw how the caregivers interacted with each of our girls and how comfortable our girls were with their teachers, i gradually became less worried and more trusting. Trusting that the caregivers and daycare as a whole will do what they say they would do—take proper care of our children.

When finding the right daycare, it is important to note that, not every daycare is in the business of taking care of children, some are simply on the business of making money. Here are some principles to guide you in making the right choice:

1. START early: don't wait until you have the baby before your start looking. Rather, start doing your research as soon as you find out

that you are pregnant, and decide that you will be needing childcare services. Reserve a slot of get on the waiting list as soon as possible. When it comes time to return to work, finding the right childcare shouldn't be one of your worries.

2. ASK Other Parents: Once you find a potential childcare center ask to speak with other parents who will be willing to share their experiences. Sometimes, it may be as simple as saying "hello" to a parent in the parking lot then asking them if they enjoy bringing their child to that particular childcare center, and for any other need-to-knows, both positives and negatives that they wouldn't mind sharing with you.

3. INTERVIEW the classroom teachers: schedule a meeting with the classroom teachers and ask questions on how childcare services are provided. Questions could range from, child-infant ratio, daily schedule and meal choices, and also if he/she enjoys her job, and why?

4. INTERVIEW the owner/director: ask about accreditations and where the childcare center stands with national, federal and local ratings, depending on your state. For example, we live in Delaware and the state goes by a star system. We don't look at any childcare center below the 5/5 rating scale. These are our children and we want the best for them.
5. COST versus Quality: research more than a couple childcare centers and compare rates. Be sure to also evaluate the quality of care based on your research.

Trusting who and where you drop off your children is great recipe to freeing your mind off worry as you look forward to those smiley faces at the end of your workday when you pick up your children.

FOUR
SINGLE WIVES AND SINGLE MOTHERS

"No matter what happens, my number one priority will always be to teach my children how to discover love."
-Linda Arrey-

AS I'VE SHARED with you previously, when Tse and I got married, he was still living in Europe. We knew we were getting into a long-distance marriage, but I can honestly say that we didn't understand the challenges that went with it. We were two busy people who enjoyed traveling the world, but when the children came, we no longer had the liberty to just up and go places like we used to. I could not just run to the store and let him watch the baby because he was miles away in another continent. Additionally, his time at home was sporadic at best. He was also eight hours ahead of me, which greatly impacted our ability to communicate. I would be preparing for bed when he was waking up and preparing for his day. We tried very hard to stay up late, or rise early in an effort to talk to each other. We wanted to make it work, so we were willing to do whatever it took. On a three-day weekend, he would fly to the US to spend time with us. We would attempt to travel as much as we could based upon our schedules, but traveling was expensive. A three day trip was not always an option for us. The back and forth and absence were challenging in many ways. The hardest part was that I missed my husband. I missed him during the sweet moments of our daughter's life, and I missed him being beside me for moments that we could be together. I can remember attending so many events that I wanted to share with him, but he was not there.

The sentiment that I remember most about our first year of marriage was a sense of loneliness. I knew that I wasn't alone. I had an amazing husband, but our circumstances for work were what they were. There were so many moments that I wanted to pick up the phone just to talk, but I did not because I knew that he was resting. In my quiet moments, I also felt frustrated because life was happening all around me, and he was not there. I can recall thinking that I didn't get married to be at home by myself, go to bed by myself, and go through the day by myself. In those moments, I realized that a conversation is not a conversation because I would have some pain in my heart that my husband wasn't there. When I did spend that twenty minutes being mad, I lost out on engaging in a quality conversation with my husband. I had to remind myself that no matter where he was, he was doing his best to be with me. I had to center myself to be reminded of the fact that he was doing what was best for us. I had to ask myself if someone told me to pack my stuff and move would I do it? Before we got married, we discussed moving and relocating, extensively. I was in the military and it would prove more difficult to just up and move. I had to be patient and understanding of how he would be impacted by such a large transition.

It's imperative that we understand the difference between getting involved with who someone is versus who we want them to become. We were two people who loved where we lived and had no desire to move. When reality hit him that he would be the one that had to move, it was also difficult for him. He had an established lifestyle, with a great job, and he was happy. He had purchased a home of his own and all of a sudden, he had to make plans to move. I had to take time to walk in his shoes if only for a moment, to understand what he was going through. I learned to be patient. Since we didn't have a lot of time together, the time that we did have deserved to be well-spent. I recognized that I needed to ensure that our quality time was productive and valuable. When we ended our phone calls, we would recognize the importance of talking about and working through things that bothered us. We wanted to do all that we could to alleviate stress on both sides.

The frustration that I felt from being alone did not get easier when we had our first daughter, Angel. My husband came home about three weeks prior to Angel's delivery. He was there for the delivery. I had a C-section, and then four days later, he had to go back overseas. I had Angel on Monday, and we came home on Thursday. My husband left on Saturday. That was one of the hardest times of my life and in our relationship. Although I did have some help, it wasn't from my husband. I wanted him there. I didn't want my husband's mother, or my mother, or my friends to help me. Although I was deeply appreciative for their love, my heart yearned to have my husband there. I was officially a single wife and now operating in the role of a single mother. It took a lot of guts and prayers to get through that time. After having a C-section, I was dealing with the pain and the recovery, and in addition to it all, I had a complicated pregnancy.

My husband did his best to be there with and for us from miles away, but nothing could replace his consistent presence. There were times when the phone calls were not enough for me. I constantly had to remind myself that he was not away by choice and that all that he was doing was for our family. I was going into work, picking up the baby and taking her to all needed doctor's appointments on my own. By the time I got home, I would do bottles and laundry, and it would easily be eleven at night before I could attempt to eat dinner. I don't question for a moment that the power of prayer is what carried us.

That period of my life gave me an insurmountable amount of respect for single mothers. My husband was not physically present, and I had the luxury of knowing that I was not responsible for doing it all alone. Whether we are single wives or single mothers, we must constantly remind ourselves to use our time wisely. We must never forget the hopes, dreams and ideals that we have for our children. In the end, when we raise children who know that they are loved and nurtured, we will help them to discover love in their hearts. Time and time again, we must remember the reasons why we do all things.

ESTABLISHING A NETWORK

ONE OF MY biggest challenges as a single wife and a single mother was attending appointments to the doctor. Taking time away from work can appear to others as unreasonable. When you're by yourself and you have no one to call, it can be disheartening. I advise working mothers to establish a support network. Establishing a group of people who can throw you a lifeline when you are floundering will give you hope that you can make it across the finished line. Establishing a community or village should not be taken lightly. Had I put more emphasis into creating that support network, it would've helped me to navigate my challenges easier ways.

It is important to note that, not all friendships are great for you. While is it good to have a support network, be mindful about not bringing negative people into your personal space. What you propel is what you attract. Spread the same vibe you want your tribe to possess.

FIVE
SLEEPING AND RESTING

"And even when a mother's eyes are closed, her ears are opened- - listening to the heartbeats of her children."
-Linda Arrey -

D O MOTHERS SLEEP? Inquiring minds want to know. My daughter didn't sleep through the night, and I began to believe that sleep was a thing of the past. I didn't know how to prepare for sleepless nights, and no matter how many times you hear about it, the impact is not real until it happens to you. Our first daughter was colicky, and wanted to nurse to be soothed. There were days I was brought to tears when I knew that she had been fed but the crying continued.

What mother doesn't want to do everything in her power to comfort her baby? When you have done all that you can and you feel as though you have no additional solutions, it breaks your heart.

I was disregarding my pain from the C-Section to attend to my baby's needs. I was also very limited to certain positions because the procedure dictated that the amount of weight that I lifted had to be considered. I had a big baby; both of our girls were big. After my first baby, I even developed an infection because I kept handling her weight. The pattern of my lack of sleep continued as my daughter would not sleep in her crib. Furthermore, she always wanted me to carry her, and I did just that. There were times when my mother would attempt to coerce me to give her the baby, and she would encourage me to eat. I wasn't sleeping or eating the way that I should have been.

On what seemed like rare occasions, my baby would finally go to sleep, but her sleeping patterns were short. After about thirty to forty minutes of sleep, she was awake again. Upon attending my six weeks appointment, my doctor said, "you're not okay." "I know, and I just haven't slept in six days," I replied. My mother-in-law was visiting at the time. My doctor recommended that I nurse the baby, then hand her over to my mother-in-law and get some sleep, even if it meant wearing earplugs. She was worried about my mental well-being. How was I supposed to wear earplugs and still hear the baby if she were to wake up? Her response was golden. "The point is so that you don't hear her." "You need to take care of yourself, so that you can take care of your child." Consumed by exhaustion and anxiety, I went home, and I did not follow the doctor's advice. The mother in me just couldn't do it.

How was I to sleep when I had a six week old baby who required my attention? It was not possible. My baby was exclusively breastfeeding, and she needed to eat. Had I known then that Dr. Lacy was right, I might have made a different decision. Rest is so important to nurture our bodies and our minds. A better plan would have been to nurse her when she woke up every forty minutes, and then go to sleep. It's important that, as mothers, we are in a good state of mind and have a good physical disposition to best provide for our children.

It got to the point that I was dazed and confused because I hadn't slept for so long. I thank God because nothing happened. Many new mothers suffer from the trauma of a lack of sleep. I encourage women to utilize all the help possible so that they can rest. Whenever possible, express your milk and give the husband the baby and go back to sleep. I had lots of friends who came in and out of our home. In retrospect, I should've utilized them more. I have come to realize that if we do not take care of ourselves, we are still neglecting the option to be the best for our children. I pray that mothers will learn to put themselves first so that they can put their best foot forward when caring for others. Even on the days that you don't want to be bothered, learn how to effectively surround yourself with people you don't' mind having in your space. Everyone is not comfortable watching your child, and those who are, can be a true blessing. Look around your house and see what needs to be done and ask for help. If someone comes to mow the lawn, that's a blessing. When someone says "let me know if there's something that I can do," don't disregard her offer. Let people help you.

When you allow the assistance of others to take the edge off, you can enjoy the process of being a mother. Learn to relax and learn to communicate with those closest to you. As for that notion of sleeping when the baby sleeps—there's no such thing. If we all sleep at the same time, when would we be able to wash bottles and get rid of diapers? I believe that when the baby sleeps, we benefit from finding ways to be productive. No matter what is happening around us, we must seek time for rest at all costs.

SIX
SELF-TALK AND AFFIRMATIVE ACTIONS

"Every mother must choose her words wisely, for she has the power to build up or tear down with a single phrase.
-Linda Arrey-

SELF-TALK

A MOTHER'S ABILITY TO affirm herself is immeasurable in impact. It is not possible to pour from an empty pitcher. Our role as the emotional foundation of our families is paramount. Understanding that how we speak to ourselves and our loved ones have lasting effects on the internal beliefs established that guide our decision making as well as our concept of self. We must let our lips speak life into every circumstance and possibility and establish words as an indicator of love.

We also need to establish strategies to move forward when we feel stagnant and past moments of despair. Our words frame our lives. What manifests on so many occasions is a result of the words that we gave power. As mothers, we must use words wisely and as tools of transformation for our families.

AFFIRMATIVE ACTION

IT IS NOT enough to simply recognize the power of speaking words that nurture our souls, we must be relentless in activating these words in our psyche. Daily affirmations are an impactful way to create transformative power in our lives and the lives of those we love and cherish.

- Day 1: I will bless my children at all times.
- Day 2: Abundance will be ever present in my home.
- Day 3: We will seize the day.
- Day 4: I trust in divine timing.

- Day 5: Peace begins within me.
- Day 6: The universe is conspiring for my benefit.
- Day 7: I have been granted every ounce of power that I need to manifest my will.
- Day 8: Good energy thrives in our home.
- Day 9: I am worthy.
- Day 10: My gratitude leads me to surplus.
- Day 11: Spiritual affluence is mine.
- Day 12: I will unwrap my gifts and talents to change lives today.
- Day 13: There shall be no limits on our love.
- Day 14: Financial freedom is our inheritance.

CONCLUSIVE THOUGHT:
Discover Happiness

"No matter how hard you search, you won't find happiness anywhere. The greatest of it lives inside of you."
—Linda Arrey—

IN YOUR QUEST to find happiness, you must understand what your likes and dislikes are. You must become one with your desires and internal motivations. If you aren't happy in your marriage, you have to do the work to find out what state you are in and why? If you are not happy with your children, you must rediscover love. If you aren't happy at work, you must find ways to use the skills that validate your gifts and talents. True happiness begins and ends with you. You are responsible for determining why you are not happy. You are responsible for discovering happiness in your heart. You are responsible for channeling joy. As much as we'd like to count on others to contribute to our happiness, joy is an inside job. Life only works for us when our decisions and actions are rooted in love. We must discover our internal sanctuary and spend time in that space. At the end of the day, our greatest desire is to see smiles on the faces of our loved ones and be ever so proud of the reflection that we see in the mirror.

CAVEAT
FROM THE OUTSIDE IN

"And when I become obsessed with bettering myself, I will have discovered love."
-Linda Arrey-

AS WOMEN, WE must trust that God is preparing us for marriage, even when we can't recognize the signs. Be encouraged to do the internal work on yourself before inviting a husband into the equation. Get yourself ready while the man that you have dreamed of finds you. Waiting, while being single, is a beautiful opportunity to learn to enjoy life on your own. It proves to be a time to discover new interests and ways to spend quality time with yourself. There are times when being alone is transformative. Taking time to listen to your internal voice and catering to your needs before serving in a capacity in which you are responsible for the needs of others can be empowering. During your waiting period, be selfish; you deserve it. Taking time to determine what we truly desire in a helpmate can prove to be invaluable. We must not turn away opportunities to work on our hearts and to heal past hurts so that we don't bring them into our sacred marriages. Getting married for the title alone will not make love last. There must be a presence of deeper connections. We can only be capable of producing a spiritual connection with others after we have created one within.

II
MANAGING EXPECTATIONS

[Society attempts to dictate the responsibilities for both men and women. Is there a difference for a man that provides financially versus one that does not?]

THINK IT'S HUMAN nature for a woman to look to the husband for financial stability. A man should take care of his family. If he's in a state of transition, such as going to school or preparing to take a leap of faith into entrepreneurship, that's different. During a time of transition, the mentality of a team player is vital. In those instances, the wife and the husband should work hand in hand to take care of the home. Communication is key in a scenario such as this. If the husband articulates that he is not bringing in any income as he is in pursuit of a specific goal, all of the cards are on the table. To the contrary, if he just decides that he no longer has a desire to work, with no prior conversation or attempt to collaborate, should a woman still be expected to respect him as she would have when he assumed responsibility for the home?

There is a stigma about women who make more money than their mate. While some men embrace this seamlessly, some men feel insecure in this scenario. We can also note countless scenarios when the woman is the breadwinner; her husband's insecurities rise to the occasion. Even in instances when a wife is doing everything in her power to honor and respect her husband, it is challenging to maintain the balance of responsibility. It's important that we do everything we can to make our spouses feel loved and respected, regardless of the situation. If he is just some deadbeat who doesn't want to work and just wants to sit at home, then that's a different story. Maybe, the wife works outside the home and the father decides that he does not wish to have the children enrolled in daycare, then that's a different story. He's doing his part. It's all about constant communication and creating that balance.

[SHOULD WIVES SUBMIT TO THEIR HUSBANDS?]

PEOPLE MAKE BIBLICAL references about wives submitting to their husbands. In my opinion, it is perfectly okay for the wife to submit to her husband. If you keep reading that same verse, the Bible talks about the husband's responsibility to care for his wife. Marriage is a trinity between the man, the woman, and God. You can't take away any parts of the triangle. When you want to talk about submission of the wife in the home, you have to talk about the man loving his wife as Christ loved the church (Ephesians 5:25).The Bible tells us that a woman should respect her husband. A man who does not bring his family close to God, or one who cheats on his wife, has no room to talk about submission. No matter how hard everyone tries, it will not work. Growing up in an African family gave me a variety of perspectives from which to draw. One thing I found interesting in the United States is a tradition where the wife's family pays for the wedding. I was shocked. Today, I'm still shocked. In my culture, if you want to marry a father's daughter, the man must show that he is financially able to provide. Don't ask an African dad to pay for a wedding. He would probably chase you down the street. I was not raised with the daughter's family assuming this role, so the concept is foreign to me.

African parents are looking for a demonstration of love and financial stability. They would say that a prospective husband should be able to care for their daughter. Why would I give you to marry my daughter? It doesn't' make sense in a traditional African culture.

We must accept the fact that roles vary from culture to culture. I am a firm believer and society reinforces the concept that men should be regarded as the head of the home. Are there any women that desire to be the head of the home? And in instances where women are the heads of the household, there are factors that contribute to this end. We are called to respect men as leaders, and I would venture to say that we expect to see men lead in this way.

[WHAT QUESTIONS SHOULD WOMEN ASK THEMSELVES PRIOR TO BEING MARRIED?]

DO I TRUST him? Is he financially irresponsible? Is he respectful? Will he love his wife? Is he capable of stepping out? Will I allow him to lead? Do I respect him? In order for a woman to follow a man, she must trust his leadership. She must trust that he is going to lead them where they should go. Some men are revered and respected but only because they have demonstrated, in merit, that they were deserving of such respect. If a woman does not share a man's vision, she will not follow. Communicating to understand personal and family needs is vital to mutual understanding.

SEVEN

CONSTRUCT A HOUSE OR BUILD A HOME?

"When we build good things, they have
a way of building us in return."
-Linda Arrey-

AS MOTHERS, OUR main goal should be to build harmonious homes, filled with love. When we focus on situations rather than people, we place valuable building blocks in place to do so. I can remember receiving a call from daycare that another kid scratched my daughter's face. I was told that there was no opened wound. On my way to the school to pick her up, I was talking to my husband, and I didn't want to focus on who had harmed our daughter? I didn't feel that who had done it was what was most important. The fact that she was hurt was what was most important to me. The details of how she was hurt were what I focused on. When I arrived at the school, I discovered that she did have an opened cut. I also learned that the other kid didn't just scratch her, but he also pushed her. None of this had been documented. It is possible that the staff at the daycare didn't see what happened; however, no one was fully aware of the details, nor did they bother to fully check her out. My daughter had a scratch on her face and bruises on her knees. I knew that my mindset would serve as the premise for how I would handle the situation. In that moment, I had the power to create harmony or wreak havoc. That day for me was packed with appointments, but I had to take care of my daughter and take care of my clients. I could've been angry and cursed people out, or I could take my daughter into my arms and show her a lot more love than the student who had hurt her or the teachers who didn't do too much. I made the decision to love her. The more love that I infused in her heart at that moment, the more comforted she was in knowing that she was safe. By the time I left, she was playing again. If I had been angry, and approached the situation with negative energy, I would have returned back to work in the wrong frame of mind. This was something that I had to learn. I used to be quick to anger and easily offended. I don't really use profanity, but I do get angry. I could've gotten upset and then not been able to give my client one hundred percent of me. I could've been so angered by the phone call that I missed the hurt my daughter had truly experienced. When we get to the place where our minds are jaded with resentment or ill will, we must remember to think about what's important and who is important. I use this same approach in our home. I never want us to get caught up in the rapture of events in our house that forces us to forget to build a home together. When we determine that the people and relationships in our home are what we value, our approach towards each other is completely different.

I could have placed value in making sure that the kid who hurt our daughter got punished, but would it have helped? They were two and three years old at the time. Far too often, we put value in punishing people when they do things that cause us hurt. And even though they are just children, we can learn a great deal from the scenario. When we begin to feel angry about things, we must ask ourselves—is that feeling adding to our lives? This question is sure to get us back to the right mindset.

Throughout my marriage, I used to get offended about everything. I expected my husband to act a certain way, and I disregarded the fact that he was a grown man that already had a certain way of doing life. I had to realize that everything I wanted is not always right. There is no right or wrong with marriage and that's okay. There are days when we value different things in different ways. What's most important is that we love and respect each other for who we are. Learning to be respectful, even if we don't agree, is a crucial step in building a home together. Reciprocity of love must never cease to exist in a home. It took me a while to realize this. I had to stop and consider that maybe there were times when my husband was feeling what I was feeling. During those times, I realized that he too was capable of having hurt feelings. To take things a step further, what if he is right? It is not possible that we are right all of the time, no matter how much we try to convince ourselves otherwise. We often try so hard to get the other person to see our point that we miss out on the opportunities to disagree in love. When we feel very strongly about what it is that we are feeling, the conversation isn't going to be progressive. No matter what we go back and forth about, what's important is a constant, and that is to care for our families. We want the same result in the end. That thought alone cancels out many of the unimportant aspects of things that we could disagree about. As I write this book, we are redoing our basement. My husband is calling all the shots. I had to recognize that I was given the opportunity to decorate the rest of the house, and when I did, I went wild without much of his input. I didn't realize that it was even possible that he wanted to have an input because he allowed me to play with the decor and arrangements in our home as I wanted. Building a home together, automatically denotes that it is not about one person. The establishment of a home that both partners love is what matters. It should be just as important that he loves our home just as I do. He's living in it as much as I am, and he loves our home as much as I do. Holy matrimony calls us to love one another and to always do all that we can to create a harmonious life, together.

EIGHT
FINANCES

*"Mothers must sow financial seeds
to reap a financial harvest."*
-Linda Arrey-

F OR MOTHERS AND families, planning is the key to financial abundance. Some of the women I encounter often say that they don't have money to invest in a business or to go on a vacation. If you have a source of income, then you have money. The way in which we manage our money is what creates opportunity. I recommend the practice of working on strategies to maximize the money we earn from our hard work.

With planning, you have to be able to allocate funds towards necessities as well as what is important to you. What are your must pay bills? What are the things you have to do for your well-being? Taking care of the must pay bills is not negotiable. In addition to the must pay bills, there are also well-being bills. Although well-being bills do not present the same level of urgency, they are important for mental and emotional sustainability. Many women never allocate funds to take care of themselves, often waiting to determine if there will be money left over after everything is paid for. There are other things to pay for, and if you didn't factor it in, that money will be spent in another place. If we allocate funds for necessities, at what point do we add self-care to the list?

In our home, we have a joint account that is used to pay bills, and individually we maintain our personal accounts. Together, we decide how much money we will allocate to our individual accounts. You don't have to do something for yourself every month, but it needs to become a commitment. If you have some money somewhere, then you have some money to put towards must have items. I believe that self-care is a must have item. You might place one hundred dollars or twenty-five dollars in your account for self-care item. Everything depends on your income and personal preferences. Whether it's planning your vacation or planning your retreat, small purchases that you don't have to discuss will come from the personal account. If you have a business together or separately, each business should have a separate account.

There should also be the presence of a joint investment account. It can be a savings account, or a tithing account. You have to discover what works for your household. I've shared this information with other couples who have tried it, and it's working for them. It is your responsibility to tell your money where it goes. The moment your money is telling you where it goes, you're not paying things you need to pay. When it comes to finances, planning is paramount. It is also possible that you have more things to pay, and your income does not adequately cover any extras. In those instances, the goal should be to prioritize based on importance and your timelines for payment. I'm no financial expert, but I don't believe in having debt.

There is no greater feeling than being debt free in America. Getting out of debt should be a top priority for your family. In a home, you and your spouse should have financial meetings, just as you would for your job. The management of your finances is a job, and you are both employed by your household to implore sound fiscal management. You are called to share your financial goals and plans together. When your kids are old enough, bring them into the discussion. Let them know about being financially responsible. The ultimate goal is to build generational wealth that spans long after your lifetime together.

NINE
EXPECTATIONS IN THE WORKPLACE

"A mother can be busy, but her best
works occur when she is productive."
-Linda Arrey-

CONSULT YOUR HEART

NO MATTER WHAT your position is in the workplace, your greatest mission is to help others feel valuable. From the implementation of programs that incentivise to kind words that build morale, you have the power to ignite purpose. As mothers, we know the power of being reminded of our value and the lasting effects that a sense of worthiness can have on our overall disposition and performance. The simple words "I love you" offered in appreciation from our children make our hearts flutter and ignite a passion to work twice as hard to make the little faces that we adore happy. This is also true of the workplace. People work hard when they feel valued and that someone recognizes their sense of purpose. You could be the reason that someone reports to work every day. You could allow your infectious positivity to invigorate hope in your place of work.

Whether at home or in the workplace, you must first understand that you deserve to be there. You aren't responsible for understanding everyone's purpose, but you are held accountable for recognizing your own purpose. When you understand your purpose, you also recognize your value and what you contribute. Your calling to nurture does not end when you leave your home. You are called to lead and to transmit hope everywhere you go.

I've answered the calling to do more and be more on several occasions. A story that touches my heart is that of a lady named Stephanie. She had once been a stellar employee whose professional ship began to sink over time. She went from being extremely reliable to reporting to work profusely tardy on a daily basis. She was becoming less effective in her role by the day. In an attempt to help discover a resolve, I determined that negative ramifications such as probation or termination would be last resorts. I began to take time to invite her into my office to ask her how I could be of service to support her in getting back on track. I learned that her personal life was spiraling out of control in the wake of a husband who no longer wanted to be a part of her life. She was now struggling to make ends meet financially and to single handedly care for the child they had conceived together. She began coming to speak with me on a daily basis as an outlet. Although I never disclosed to anyone what she had encountered, I also went as far as to assist her financially on one occasion, from my own finances. My heart compelled me to do so, and that was all the reassurance that I needed. Over time, the small doses of love made a difference. Stephanie ended up coming to work on time. Although I am not an advocate of divorce, it appeared that a weight was lifted off her shoulders after she finalized her separation from a marriage that no longer served her. She began to take more pride in herself while practicing consistent acts of self-care. She had let herself go in so many ways when she felt undervalued and unappreciated. I thanked God for her growth and for allowing me to possess resources, both fiscal and spiritual, to be of assistance.

Today, Stephanie is at a place where she is embracing being single. She found a home for her heart at a church, and her self-confidence is soaring. Stephanie no longer needs daily sessions in my office, and I have since filled the time with other tasks from my growing list of things to accomplish. I am beyond proud to say that she does not need me in the capacity that I once served, because she has discovered her voice and her happiness.

MRS. CEO

WE ARE STILL amidst a society that is uncomfortable with women being in positions of leadership. As much as people pretend that women leading is acceptable and welcomed, there is a vast population of people who beg to differ. I've been in a lot of board meetings where I was astounded at the makeup of the room. I can recall on occasions, sending a text message to my husband or my brother, who is one of my biggest mentors or even a girlfriend, to say that in a room filled with leaders, I was the only woman. In many instances, I was the only woman of color. I know that I am a good worker but there are lots of good workers. There are so many of us out there, why would I be the only one in the room?

My strong personality seems to keep some of the non progressive thought processes at bay, but I know that they do exist. I made a decision to not allow anyone to take anything away from me. Everything that I have, I have earned. When I walk into a room, I command the room and the proper respect. I've had people try to change me, but after a few trials, I think they realize that I am not the one. Also recently learned of the phrase RBF (you can look it up), referred to women who don't smile in meetings or have a 'certain look.' The question then goes: How often are men asked to smile, otherwise labeled, based on the look on their faces in meetings?

As working mothers we have to equip ourselves to be strong in our credentials and experiences, so that our presence speaks for itself in the boardroom. We have every right to be present.

BE CONFIDENT

OUR ACCOMPLISHMENTS SHOULD read such that we can walk in confidence because we deserve to be in any given professional scenario. Confidence should radiate in your face and through your actions.

As a working mother, you have many reasons to be confident. The greatest is all that you have been tasked with managing. I've had many first days in my career. We must be strong, confident and prepared at all times. You must find ways to stay on top of your game so that you solidify your presence and your confidence. No one can take away what you have rightfully earned. When you have internal confidence because you have done the work to be in the position that you are in, no one else's opinion matters. Your belief in yourself is not something that you need to communicate verbally, it shows up in your smile and the way you talk. It is important to note that confidence does not equate to arrogance. We can be both confident and humble at the same time.

As working mothers, we are well equipped to wear multiple hats. Just because you are a mother or a working mother doesn't mean you can't be an entrepreneur as well. Statistics show that women are better with financials. Even so, women still make less money than men in corporate America. That's another conversation for another time but noteworthy and terribly unequal.

It is my belief that if a woman decides to leave her home to work for someone else, she must leave with her armor on. We must never conform to the notion that it is permissible for women to make less, whey they are performing in the same roles as our male counterparts. We should equip ourselves in such a way that we can come to the table and negotiate what we are worth. We must also actually have something to document our negotiating power and to nullify whatever society has set forward. More importantly, we cannot fall into the trap of demonstrating the stereotypes that affect the rationale behind women getting paid less. Be educated, have your certifications in place, and back your arguments with you experience. Ensure that you skill set qualifies you for the job, so that when you come before the board or a potential employer, you have no need to conform to the salary they offer you. You have every right to own what you are bringing to the table. Don't be shy, make demands that are in your best interest. Don't be afraid to overstep the confines of the box that society attempts to place you in. When you are qualified, you deserve to be your biggest advocate in the workplace. If you don't stand up for the work that you have executed to be at the top of your game, who will? Who will stand up for women to get what they deserve in the workforce? The change that we wish to see in the world, begins within each of us.

TEN
TIME MANAGEMENT

"The way we use our time teaches us a great lesson about what we believe to be most important."
-Linda Arrey-

THE ONE THING that we won't get any more of is time. As you progress in your career and your children get older, you need to get things done—Like now.

Time management is something I've always put into practice. I challenge myself to find creative ways to distribute my time. My main objective is to be in control of my time as opposed to allowing it to control me. I am aware of all the things that I need to accomplish in a day. I am also aware of the fact that I need eight hours of sleep. I personally don't function well when I don't get enough sleep.

I believe this to be true for many of us, whether we choose to admit it or not. I've heard people say that "sleep is for suckers." Nothing could be further from the truth. A lot of business owners and entrepreneurs shy away from admitting that they need rest.

IS SLEEP FOR SUCKAS?

SOCIETY PROMOTES A culture that subscribes to the mentality that you have to burn the midnight oil to be successful. If you practice effective time management, you will not have to lose sleep. When you sleep properly, you will be more effective, and you won't be as irritable. It's very important to understand and practice effective management of your time. In all things, we should set goals. Part of my goal setting is using my twenty-four hour time allocation to the fullest. The goals that we set for how we use our time should be smart goals. When we set smart goals, we don't set ourselves up for failure. It is imperative that you know what your capabilities are and what you can complete within a given time frame.

If you feel you need to allocate ten hours for your work day to accomplish what you need to get done, don't set yourself up for failure by allotting seven hours because it looks better on paper. Establish what is attainable. No one understands your potential and your family dynamics like you do. You must assume responsibility for setting the standard for what needs to be done.

In all of your goal setting, there must be a plan for execution. At the end of the day, try completing your schedule for the next day. Review what you have accomplished, celebrate the small wins and update your list of daily tasks. This is a plan of action; however, if there is one thing that motherhood teaches us, it is that things don't always go according to plans. There are times where I come to work, and I don't get to touch the items on my list. Things happen, and that's okay. At least by having a plan, you have a blueprint to refer back to when open slots of time become available.

I also use a daily management board that helps me to keep the items that need to be done front and center. You can apply the same principle at home. Consider adding what you have to do for your children during the week to your management board.

WHAT'S FOR DINNER?

DURING THE HOLIDAYS, my mother would cook three meals a day. There were twenty people under one roof. She was a master at managing her time. It sounds unreal, but it was truly what happened in our home. My Mom actually cooked three meals a day for twenty people every single day. In my home, I don't cook every day. Although I believe that my cooking is better than the restaurant, I don't have the time or the strength to cook every day. When we do go out to eat as a family, it is more about allocating time to spend together, not for the food. I mainly cook on the weekends. I buy food in bulk to save time. I know that if I don't buy in bulk, it increases my chances of having to run to the store on a whim. I most often prepare

African food and it takes several hours. There is no a fifteen-minute meal prep for me on those occassions. To save time, I block hours to go grocery shopping on Saturdays. At this time, I shop for the whole week. I also cook in large portions to ensure that there is enough food for everyone. On the days that I cook, I often prepare sides. Another way that I manage my time is setting time aside for laundry. We have two little ones and we do quite a bit of laundry. I must admit that my husband is better at cleaning the house than I am. He also does the laundry more frequently. We budget for a housekeeper as needed. My goal is to plan the entire weekend before it arrives. I look at the weather and make a determination about what we can accomplish during that time. There are some weekends that we don't do anything. On other occasions, it's good to take the kids out to the park, or the beach. We do what we can to keep them entertained.

WHAT'S YOUR END GOAL?

THE MOST IMPORTANT lesson for us to remember regarding time management is that not everything is a priority. I can't emphasize this enough. Just because you have to get it done doesn't mean you have to get it done right now. That's something that every mother should keep in mind. Many times we overbook our schedules because we are attempting to prioritize too much. If you accept the fact that you can't do it all today, then you would be forced to analyze what is realistic in the time that you have.

Set deadlines for items that you do not yet have finalized. If you have more pressing activities that you need to direct your attention towards, put everything else aside and get those things done. This strategy helps you to not become overwhelmed. This scenario can lead to stress, and who needs stress? A working mother is the last person who needs to concern herself with activities that don't add to her quality of life. It's very important to be stress free, because you have so many counting on you. I'm not saying that you should leave a messy house, but if you have a little laundry that you have not been able to get to, put it in the laundry room and come back to it later. Always remember to ask yourself, what is the end goal?

It is possible that you need the two hours that you could have completed laundry in to put your feet up and get some rest.

PLAN TO SUCCEED

BE FOCUSED AND be flexible. Even when things don't work out, you must take comfort in knowing that you did everything in your power to stick to that plan. You cannot let all the things that are outside of your control affect your abilities. Plan to succeed at all costs. Never forget your potential but do know that there is no merit in overwhelming yourself. Things happen, and there are times when you have to abort the plan. The end goals will not change.

If you keep going and keep implementing these skills, tools and strategies, you will get there. You can't get frustrated along the way and say it's not working. You must not quit, and you must put in the time to ignite these strategies in your everyday life. Once effective time management becomes a part of your lifestyle, you will see long lasting results. Be patient with the process until it becomes a part of you.

ELEVEN
MOTHERHOOD AND BEING IN BUSINESS

"An effective CEO in the home is an
effective CEO in the business."
-Linda Arrey-

I'S IMPORTANT FOR mothers to create alternate sources of incomes. Not relying on one paycheck that comes at the end of the month can prove to be rewarding in many ways. Establishing a business can provide you with an unrestricted opportunity to use your gifts and talents in ways that stimulate your mind and establish an identity outside of your husband and children. Using your personal time to think about how you can use your God-given talents to create another source of income, is time well spent. Take time to reflect upon your job and ask yourself if this is where I want to be. If you have not reached your final destination, create a plan of action that establishes a path to get where you want to be. After engaging as a wife and a mother, we often forget that we can do so many other things. The greatest resource of man is man. We build the machines that we so often fear we will be replaced by. Many working mothers are naturally creative. When given the time to just sit down and think about the skills that we have, our possibilities become endless. You have to find a way to host your own personal episode of Shark Tank and pitch your business idea to yourself. If you are still stuck on how to launch a new endeavour, seek out a professional coach, whose goal is to help you create an alternate source of income. Having that autonomy to run yourself is powerful. There are times that it is not about the money and more so about the ability to create something larger than yourself.

MOTHER. BOSS. VISIONARY.

I ADVOCATE FOR mothers to establish alternate sources of income. Not everybody wants to be a millionaire. Whatever your comfort level is for your family, you have to ask yourself if the money you bring in every month is gratifying to you.

I am in no way, shape or form against working a job, but I am an advocate of working mothers becoming entrepreneurs. I'm not saying that it is wise to quit your nine to five to start a business. I am saying that there are hidden benefits in both opportunities that we don't always take advantage of. Use your job to fund your dream. Learn all that you can on the job so that your skills are transferable while running your business.

The current state of society makes it seem as if working for somebody else or a company is wrong. Have you seen the cost of healthcare in America? Many are employed for healthcare benefits alone, and there is nothing wrong with that. Don't let anybody make you feel like working employment is a bad thing. Use your career to fund your business until it is financially sufficient on its own.

HOBBIES AND BUSINESS ARE NOT CREATED EQUAL

I'VE ALSO COME across a lot of entrepreneurs who refuse to look for another job when finances are not up to par with business. There is no harm in getting a job that will sustain you after having taken the leap of faith towards entrepreneurship. People should understand that we all reserve the right to differentiate passion from business. If we are in business as a hobby, that means that you have to have a passion for it and that you love it, but your ultimate goal is not to make money. This would not be something that you invest all of your money in. Without proper market research, you have not yet established a demand. Consider your grandmother's soup as an example. You may believe it to be phenomenal, but due to a lack of marketing, nobody buys it. Two years is a good rule of thumb to see if your revenue generating activity is working or not. Place emphasis on how you can attack the market from new angles and what resources should be invested to do so. If you're going on five years and still not making a profit, break it. A loss over this amount of time, denotes a hobby. It is not results-oriented to love a product more than your customers love it. This is a mistake I see in a lot of entrepreneurs. They were so in love with their product, and they silenced what the customers had to say. If the majority of your customers say you have too much salt in the soup, you should listen. You can't get angry when a customer has an opinion. As an entrepreneur, you have to look at what your customer wants. If you are creating products and services that you love more than your clients, then you have a hobby, not a business. When you set out to create a business, your goal is to serve a purpose, serve a particular niche, and to make money. If you're not generating revenue within three to five years, then you must restructure your strategy. It is possible that the nature of your business denotes a longer period of time to yield income. At the outset of your business, the goal is to generate revenue, but to also make enough money to run your business. To make money, you should be able to research what your clients need, want and desire.

STRUCTURE

ESTABLISHING ON PAPER what problem your business solves as well as what services you will be offering, and who your targeted audience is, proves to be essential to the process. Also taking time to determine what you need in terms of money and resources to start is key.

It is equally important to legalize your business. The most common forms of businesses are sole proprietorships. You can also consider structuring a partnership or corporation. Many small businesses, opt for a Limited Liability Company (LLC). You can always register your business with the state by going to the Secretary of State's website. Be sure to obtain an Employee Identification Number (EIN) from the Internal Revenue Services (IRS) for identification and tax purposes.

When it comes to finances, my advice is that you separate your business account from all personal accounts and do business with your business accounts. It's best to structure your business separately from your personal finances. Starting up your business, it is likely that you're not going to pay yourself or any employees. The best way to get free labor is to offer internships to students or volunteers. This establishes a mutually beneficial relationship because you are investing in your interns and volunteers and grooming them for future endeavours, while they assist with the growth of your business.

Your long term goals should be outlined in your business plans. You've served as the CEO of your home, why not transfer those skills into an entity that can yield additional sources of income for both you and your family? You are worth every single penny!

BEFORE YOU LEAP

BECOMING AN ENTREPRENEUR is never easy. And it's not as glamorous as most people make it look on social media, especially during the early days.

I'm not your regular entrepreneur. I have a nine to five (more accurately seven thirty to five) career as an Active Duty Officer in the U.S. Air Force. I love my career and enjoy serving in the world's greatest military.

My biggest challenge as an entrepreneur and working mother who is not on a quest to terminate her employment, is finding the time.

Spending quality time with family remains my priority; I'm sure it's yours also. As I allocate time for work and business, family must come first. There are days I have to switch things around, but family remains on the top of my scale of preference.

It is also easy to say I don't have time to take on additional clients, I don't have time to do that one thing I know fully well is what I need to do to scale my business and up-level. However, we have to adopt the mindset that the best time to take action is now. As I have shared with you previously, always remember that not everything is a priority, and some things can wait.

Some key principles as a young entrepreneur starting out is to first identify your WHY, then answer some significant, yet basic questions:

1. WHAT need/problem are you solving?
2. DO you have the necessary knowledge, passion and skill set for the industry you are venturing into?
3. WHO is your targeted audience?
4. WHO are your competitors?
5. WHAT about you and your business sets you apart from your competitors?

6. WHO are the leaders in your industry?

Expect challenges, they will come. It simply means you are at the verge of a breakthrough and expansion.

There are days that you may feel like giving up when you are not getting desired results. I say if you are putting in your best work, trust the process and be patient. Don't compare your first month in business to your competitors five years in business. Be positive and remain consistent.

Also, find a mentor or Coach in the industry you are venturing into. It is very essential to a solid foundation.

I believe every entrepreneur thinks about giving up at least once. I know because I've been there. It is a great phase to go through because you come out better and stronger. You figure out areas that need improvement and new causes of action. Celebrate the fact that you had this moment. It only gets better from here.

4 TRUTHS TO ACCEPT BEFORE BECOMING AN ENTREPRENEUR

1. DON'T Give Up. Before you get started, it is imperative that you construct a mindset that is built to endure. Entrepreneurship is no easy feat but so worth your while. You will learn so many things about yourself and achieve goals that you never even knew possible. Your patience will be tested and there will be times that you want to throw in the towel. Whatever you do, don't quit. Your reward shall soon come.

2. YOU Must Know Your Strengths and Weaknesses. The only way to be your absolute best is to know the areas that you are most effective in. It is of equal importance to discover attributes for further development. To be a lifelong learner means to discover new information, and to be innovative in your approach to the problems that your business solves for others.

3. IF You Don't Have Fun, It Won't Be Fun. Finding the joy in the business that you have set out to create is one of the many benefits of embarking upon the entrepreneurial journey. Doing the things that you are most passionate about and discovering ways to generate a profit for it can yield happiness. From collaborations to the establishment of new partnerships, building a business can be so much fun. The goal is to not get so inundated with tasks that you miss the treasure of venturing out in the land of the unknown.
4. YOUR Circle of Influence Matters. From friends to family to cohorts and new acquaintances, the demands of entrepreneurship establish a need to have people in your corner like never before. Having witnesses to attest to your greatness and support for your heart during the moments that you need to be reinforced of your worth are crucial to your ability to sustain. Nothing monumental was ever

achieved in isolation. And while you don't need people to validate you, it is always beneficial to know that you are not in the world alone when you set out to achieve your goals.. It is equally important to understand that not everyone has to go with you into your season of greatness. Abram had to part ways with Lot before God gave him the promised land (Genesis 13:14-17). People who bring negativity, occupy space in your life and block your blessings, keeping you away from what God has in store for you. Don't feel guilty about your decision to end negative relationships and those that don't add value to your life.

TWELVE
THINGS NO ONE EVER TOLD YOU

*"We are all destined to learn
something for the first time."*
-Linda Arrey-

AS A NEW mother, I relied quite a bit on a doctor named Google. I was desperately trying to figure out resources that could teach me what I didn't know. Children don't come with instructional manuals. And while internet based sources are so helpful, you can read so much that you develop information overload. If you research something enough, you can also find conflicting information that confuses you beyond measure. It is possible that even your pediatrician says something that does not sit well with you and leads you back to Dr. Google. What do you do with all of the information that you have aquired? Can anyone else really tell you everything that is best for your child? I resolve to say "no". At the end of the day, making sure your child is taken care of and safe is a mother's top priority.

My biggest fear was Sudden Infant Death Syndrome (SIDS). I'm a light sleeper to begin with, but for months, I slept on the edge of the bed, listening for my baby's breathing. I would position the crib so that I could see everything. I woke up constantly to check on the baby. My husband has seen me at night hovering over the baby monitor. During those moments that my husband would be at home, he would speak out of concern and ask if I were okay. He could sense my fear.

Much of my concern was because my daughter did not sleep. I would put her down, and as soon as her back would hit the bottom of the crib, she was wide awake. By the time I returned to work, my baby was still not sleeping, and my anxiety continued to grow. SIDS was not something that I had heard about prior to becoming a parent. My parents put me on my stomach to sleep, and it clearly worked for me. All of the information that is out, tell us not to put babies on their stomachs until they are over a year old. I was conflicted. In my culture, the women put babies on their stomachs.

I couldn't help but wonder if they did it for us and we survived, would this be impactful with my own child? I was both fearful and confident the first night that I put my child on her stomach. She was four or five months old and that was the best sleep she ever had. I watched her sleep, and I was so relieved that she finally had a good night's sleep. We were both deserving of one. My fear of SIDS didn't go away, but I found comfort in knowing that my baby was finally resting and resting well. Eventually, I got some rest too. When we transitioned her into a bassinet by our bed. I could hear her breathe, and it gave me great comfort.

No matter how much you go by the book and adhere to the information presented by the experts, there are times that you have to parent with your own instincts. And while I don't recommend that anyone go against the scientifically based information, I do recommend discovering methods that work for your children and your family.

The information on the internet was helpful for me in understanding that the older my baby got, the occurrences of SIDS dropped. I would celebrate every month my child crossed the finish line of another milestone.

"Oh my God, their percentages of SIDS is greatly reduced," I would proclaim in excitement. All mothers have different fears, but the potential of the loss of life was something that I did not take lightly. I'm thankful to say that we made it past that phase, and I would go on to worry about something else. Seemingly, a mother's worry never ends.

FEAR OF FALLING SHORT

AS YOU TRY to go by the book to give your child the best, being ever so careful to give the recommended amount of nutrition, time and love is an ongoing concern. We try so hard to live within the parameters of the box of parenting that we forget to listen to what our children are communicating. We put so much additional stress on ourselves because we love our children, and we want them to be okay, but how does doing so help us to be better parents? Some days you really question if you are being the best mom that you can be, and on other days, you flirt with feelings of failure.

I don't think that there is a mother alive who has never asked herself if she was failing? There are times when we beat ourselves up for being gone too long from our children, whether for work or because we have embarked upon a self-imposed break. Those added pressures that we put on ourselves have a tendency to well up, deep down in our hearts, and cause us concern. No matter what happens, we must never forget that the most important thing we can do for our children is love them. The act of acting in love is the reason that we were granted the privilege of becoming their parents. Finding ways to communicate in love is the answer that we so desperately search for. No amount of information online can reinforce the ways in which we must love our children. We must treat our kids in such a way that they never question our love for them. Doing so should relieve us of the extra stress associated with questioning our parenting and the fear of losing a child or a child being hurt.

My good friend and colleague, Winnie O. once shared with me that we are not fully loving our children until we recognize and accept that our children are not ours. She went on to say that "Our children belong to God, and we are here to serve as guardians of God's children." Her most powerful message stayed with me and helped me to realize that the ultimate peace of mind is knowing that our children are covered in the blood and protected. We must remember to dedicate our kids to God and rest assured that they are in his hands. We must trust that he will protect them. If we trust in God and really believe that we are the keepers of God's children, we will never have to walk in fear. We cannot fail them if we are righteous in our job to love them.

CHILDCARE

THE GREAT DEBATE about childcare will likely never end. There are many mothers who don't believe that anyone else should assume responsibility for the care of children, while another sector of mothers believe that there are no other options when mothers have to work. I stand firmly in the middle of the debate. I would rather be in the presence of my children at any given moment than apart on every day of the week. I wish that I did not need childcare, but as a working mother, the reality is that I do. It is my greatest joy to get back to them. For mothers who do need a break after a long day of work, take it. No one should be able to decide what equation works for you and your family. I want to spend time with my kids. The truth is that I work, and I need to be at my place of work, during designated hours. I look to the professionals at my daughter's schools to be a part of the support system that I have established for my family and me to raise our children.

The greatest form of childcare is established within the collaborative efforts that you and your husband establish. Remaining in constant communication about how you can help each other lightens the load in so many ways. It is equally important to ensure that each partner, who is responsible for childcare, feels valued. When you feel valued, the kids see that value, and they learn to appreciate it.

THIRTEEN
MIND OVER MATTER

"The strongest muscle a mother can exercise is her mind."
-Linda Arrey-

AS A WORKING mother, we're already balancing enough responsibility worthy of a superhero cape. We have to be accountable for the kids, our spouses, work, and ourselves. The only way to endure is with the right mindset. When our plates are full, it is not hard to become overwhelmed and stressed. Creating an environment where a positive mindset abounds can be the saving grace that we deserve. The right mindset positions us so that we don't take things so seriously. If we were brutally honest with ourselves, we would discover that there are so many factors outside of our control, and getting angry about your husband not putting the toilet seat down is so minor in comparison to being concerned about the health and welfare of your family.

Why do we allow those little things to have such an impact on our disposition? When we dig beneath the surface, we discover that many of the things that consume our positive energy are things that don't really matter. Having the right mindset and focusing on the end goal, is where we must direct our attention at all times.

We must also make it a consistent practice to understand our feelings and the root causes of them. When you have a laundry list of things to do and you're stressed, the only person that is really upset is usually you. Does being angry actually get anything of merit accomplished? Let the church say "Amen". Acting amidst frustration only disrupts your home and creates hostility in the place that has been designated as a peaceful sanctuary. Hostility and frustration also hinder your ability to get things done well.

INTENTIONAL HARM VS. CAREFREE LIVING

KEEP IN MIND that your family loves you. They don't want you to be angry or upset. Instead of being upset that your husband left the seat up, just put it down and move on to doing the things that you care about. This is an example of using your mind to avoid unnecessary stress. Try to be emphatic by walking in the shoes of another because it places you in a position of empowerment when you see things from other angles.We create problems in our minds that are nonexistent and those that welcome frustration into our spaces.When you get frustrated with your one year old, is she always aware of what she has done wrong, or is she somewhere between pushing boundaries and teachable moments? What does she know? When you consider the fact that children are designed to push the envelope of comfort so that they can learn and their minds can be developed through experience, you can easily recognize that they don't always mean harm. Considering things from this perspective reminds you that you should be loving your baby and taking care of your baby. This same strategy must remain consistent in the workplace. How do we benefit when we are angry with a colleague at work? The right mindset helps you to remain grounded in your value and self-worth. No one has the qualifications necessary to be you; only you can be you. Know what you bring to the table and remain confident in it. Taking special care to empower the people that add value to your life is another example of exercising mental strength. Those that don't add value to your life deserve little to none of your attention, let go of them at all costs.

CHANGE THE NARRATIVE

AS MOTHERS, WE are conditioned to protect and to serve. It is often easy to think the worst of every situation before we consider the good. I established a Facebook group for working mothers, purposed to change the narrative. Through the discussions, I challenged mothers to consider scenarios in which they thought that another person's intention were good before bad. I am calling for us to change the way that we approach our relationships. Let's first see the good in people.

There is enough bad in our world, but we need to know that the sunshine exists.

Having the right mindset can change your life completely. The way that we see the world and ourselves in it, changes the way we carry ourselves, our approaches to those we love, our business and our day to day interactions with people. It's imperative that we have the right mindset at all times. In the end, you are the one with the greatest power. You are in control of your disposition.

III.
CHANNELING LOVE

[WHAT IS THE ULTIMATE DISPLAY OF LOVE?]

HAD TO REALIZE that everything I want is not always what's right. I've learned over the years that there is no right or wrong in marriage. It's okay to create your own destiny for your relationship and not subscribe to societal imposed ideals of what a marriage is supposed to be. There are days when we inevitably value different things. What's important is that we love each other for what we each value and respect, even if we don't agree. The ultimate display of love is yielding to the needs of the person you love. As mothers, we do so on a continual basis. It almost seems as if it is instinctual for a mother to place the needs of the family before her own. We must then consider how to love our spouses.

When we find ways to place the needs of others before our own, we ignite a spark of love that becomes contagious, and it is reproduced within our home over and over again. Love is taught and can most profoundly be seen through action.

[WHAT MAKES US AFRAID TO LOVE?]

LOVE MAKES US vulnerable. In many instances, we don't want to lay it all on the line for fear of being rejected. We are not always sure how we will be received when we love. And although we know that we have no control over those factors, we still find ourselves afraid of being hurt. We often fear the unknown because we have no way to control it. When you give your heart to your spouse or your children or even friends or family, you don't know if it's going to be protected. We need to change the narrative. Once you have the right mindset, you put in your best and you expect nothing but the best in return. When you believe in the healing and transformative power of love, you know that love is the one emotion that conquers all. Keeping love at the epicenter of your relationship is the only way to give your whole heart. There can be no evidence of profound love in the absence of a heart. We must give all that we have to those that we love, they deserve every ounce of what we possess to give to them.

FOURTEEN
SELF-LOVE

"If you love yourself, you will know what you deserve."
-Linda Arrey-

IT'S VERY EASY to think about the kids, work, and about the husband and forget about yourself. Three months had gone by after having our first daughter, when I looked down on my feet and realized that I had not had a pedicure in several months. The demands of a new baby and adjusting to a new routine had made me neglect myself, and I did not feel good about it. Getting my nails done was not a priority at the time, but it is best practice to factor time to love you into your schedule.". It is best practice to factor time to love you into your schedule. As a mother, you need time that is dedicated to nurturing your needs. Many mothers fail in this category. Taking care of me was something that I had to learn and to start doing. If you need help taking care of your children, there should be no guilt associated with getting a nanny, if that's your thing.

I now have a routine that consists of self-care. On those days, I will get my nails done and treat myself to the spa. Afterwards, I go and sit and just eat ice cream. After my ritual concludes, I am re-energized to go home and prepare dinner. Mentally, my mind is relaxed, and I feel rejuvenated. On those days, we also have a longer family time. When you are mentally energized and fulfilled, you are more energetic at work and at home to attend to the needs of others. For some women, the opportunity to attend to self might consist of going to the mall or taking a day trip. No matter what is on your list of things to do, your name should be among the top. It is also important to note when to practice self-love. The goal is to be empowered to give from a place of overflow, not emptiness.

Not only do working mothers deserve quality time with ourselves, but we also deserve quality time with our spouses. My husband and I do a lot of dates when our children are at daycare. A small visit to the movies or an intimate lunch together can prove to be the perfect opportunity to reconnect amidst busy lives with the children.

It is also imperative that you make sure that your spouse is engaging in self-care moments too. I'm probably one of those women who is too attached to my husband. Even so, I recognize that we both have a need for individual time to nurture ourselves.

You also need time to connect intimately with your kids. One on one time with your child can be a source of great joy. In our children, we are blessed to see a part of ourselves. Those are all independent factors that bring strength to the family as a unit. When women speak about how empty, drained or overwhelmed they are, I immediately recognize a need for time to love self. I hear a lot of women who say they feel empty or they have nothing left to give. If you are feeling empty, you need to communicate with your spouse or a loved one with whom you can speak to freely and who has your best interest at heart. Locate a judgement free zone and take some time for yourself. Almost three months had gone by after giving birth to Angel, before I realized that I hadn't done my nails or hair in a while. I was focused on caring for our little princess. I finally stopped to look at my toes, and I knew that it was time for Mommy to get pampered. On that same day, I also decided to get a massage. Self-care is not optional, as we seek to care for those that we love.

10 RANDOM ACTS OF SELF-CARE

1. TAKE a relaxing bath.
2. WEAR your favorite perfume.
3. GO outside and watch the sky.
4. BUY yourself some flowers.
5. DO something for the first time.
6. CLEAR your calendar for an afternoon and plan to do nothing.
7. DANCE to your favorite song.
8. PLAN to catch up with a supportive friend.
9. SIT in silence.
10. WRITE yourself a letter of love.

Taking care of your physical, mental and spiritual well-being is a must, not an option. Speaking words infused with power over your life is one of the most effective ways to remind yourself of your strengths and to boost your confidence during those moments when self-doubt shows up. Insecurity, doubt, anxiety and any other factor that seeks to suppress our joy is not yours to own. Speak prosperity and power into your life.

10 I AM STATEMENTS EVERY MOTHER MUST SPEAK

1. I AM A Queen.
2. I AM Compassionate.
3. I AM Brilliant.
4. I AM Happy.
5. I AM Confident.
6. I AM Free.
7. I AM Intentional.
8. I AM Courageous.
9. I AM Present.
10. I AM Enough.

SELF-CARE ON A DIME FOR THE WORKING MOTHER

SELF-CARE DOES NOT always have to be financially taxing. Quality time spent rejuvenating is meant to be meaningful but you don't have to break the bank to do so. Get into these cool ideas for showing yourself some love.

1. MEDITATE
2. LISTEN to White Noise.
3. CREATE a Bucket List.
4. APPRECIATE Nature.
5. VISIT a library.
6. LIGHT a candle.
7. LISTEN to music - Dance.
8. CREATE a fun vision board.
9. EAT well.
10. COUNT your blessings.

7 WELL CHECK QUESTIONS EVERY MOM MUST ASK HERSELF

WE TAKE OUR children to the doctor to receive their well-checks on a regular basis, but who checks on mom? We must learn to check-in with ourselves periodically to ensure that we are happy, healthy and engaged in self-love.

1. DO you get enough water?
2. DO you make time for meaningful relationships?
3. DO you get enough rest?
4. DO you eat well?
5. DO you laugh often?
6. DO you get inspired?
7. DO you feel peaceful?

FIFTEEN
MENTAL HEALTH

"Every mother faces an internal battle
that the world knows nothing of."
-Linda Arrey-

MENTAL HEALTH IS a topic that is dear to my heart. In 2017, my charity Women in Leadership Development and Empowerment, Inc. launched the *Take A Stand campaign*. The campaign brings leaders, legislators and community members together to discuss a lot of the issues regarding sexual assault and harassment in the community. Many other discussions are focused on the suicide rate. One of our pertinent topics emphasizes the need for conversations surrounding mental health concerns, resources and legislation. We examine how we can positively impact the community. Our goal is to immobilize people in support of victims and to provide resources for them. People are dying from suicide as a result of their mental health. Youth are in need of mental health counseling.

There are still many people who don't know about the term, mental health. Many think of people in a mental facility who are in need of support to live from day to day. The term means so much more, and our approach to educate must be broad in nature. We all have a need to exercise strategies that assist us in maintaining sound mental health practices. No one is exempt because the need for mental health services is a concern for many of our families. There is no person who is exempt. From the new mother to that mother who is experiencing postpartum depression months after having her baby. Consider the mother who is experiencing feelings of being overwhelmed and filled with anxiety, or the mother that is trying to balance work and home and battling stress. These are both examples of working mothers who can benefit from mental health support. Although not widely categorized, stress is a mental health concern. As we face real life, we increasingly understand that it is tough, and we all need ways to cope with what we endure on a daily basis. The concept of mental health encapsulates the notion that we have to work to remain mentally healthy. We do not remain of sound mind by simply waking up in the morning. The more that we address the topic, the more that we can tackle the battle as a cohesive society.

A significant challenge in the mental health spectrum is that many people with mental health concerns don't realize that they are suffering. Mental health concerns are not limited to a person who can't comprehend life to the extent they have to be checked into a facility. We are walking around the world daily and in need of support. We all believe that we can just deal with the hardships that come our way. It's important to understand that when you get to the point where you can't handle a situation on your own, there is the prospect of help that is available to each of us. We must never disregard the cries from the inside that no one can see.

When I had my first baby, no amount of classes or pre-birth preparations could have helped me to be ready for life postpartum. I deserve to go and get my sixty dollar check that I paid for the classes that I took back, because I didn't see the benefits. After giving birth to my daughter, the lack of sleep, trying to establish a breastfeeding relationship, and the loneliness in the absence of my husband brought on a great deal of undue stress. When I went back for my two week appointment, I hadn't slept for six days. I felt like I was losing it. I felt like I couldn't comprehend anything. My doctor had no idea at the time, but she saved me in so many ways. On that day, she simply listened to me as I expressed the sentiments in my heart. My appointment was for fifteen minutes, but I was in her office for forty-five minutes. Motherhood had changed me. There were times that I felt overwhelmed. I was so stressed that I was questioning myself. I was questioning my ability to parent. I was fortunate to have my friend Ruth N., who had just had a baby. When we were up those late nights nursing, we would call each other or send messages to each other. I had somebody that I could talk to.

I really appreciated having those opportunities to talk. In retrospect, they are what got me through. I was so open because I trusted the people with whom I talked to. I trusted that I could open up and talk about my stress in a non-judgemental scenario.

Today, society is not as accepting of the fact that mental health concerns actually exist. When we express our concerns, people tend to look at us differently. "I'm seeing a therapist" is not the most popular statement. When your immediate circle is not accepting of what you are going through, or they don't notice any of the signs that you feel lost, you can feel isolated and disconnected. If you're inner circle is not accepting, you are not comfortable enough to voice what you are going through.

It's important that when people voice their concerns, we don't turn them away. Even when people express that they are stressed, we must learn to ask how we can be of assistance to them?

We are taking mental health for granted. You might not even be the person to help, but you may be the person to hold their hand and let them know that somebody else in the world cares and is willing to listen. We have got to do a better job at protecting each other at all costs.

We must begin to ask ourselves, as a society, how we can help? We have to be vigilant of those around us. If you feel suspicious that the tone of your friend is different or that she is drinking more to cope, it could be cause for concern. There are so many signs that we miss. Ask your friends and loved ones if they are okay? Ask critical questions to check on them in a deeper way. Your goal is to gain their trust and make it okay for them to come talk to you. Establish a judgement free zone and offer any help that you can. People don't want to be looked at differently. They want to be the same person that they were before they opened up to you. Human beings are by nature very judgmental, so when we deal with critical issues like depression and people are already at the edge of suicide, we have to take off that judgmental hat and show love, care and kindness. We have to find resources that can really help. That's it. Everyone does not need professional help; some people just need a friend.

IDENTIFY YOUR WHY?

AS MOTHERS, IT is important to identify our reason for existence and our purpose. We must go far beyond the surface to discover these answers. You must discover your why. My children are my reason why. They are the reason I do everything that I do. They are beside me, living in God's purpose. Inevitably, your mind will take you to a place that causes you to question your worth. It is imperative that you know your why during these trials. Know what you seek to accomplish in life and what you plan to do to get there. We must make a conscious decision to control what goes on in our heads to the best of our abilities.

The story of world renown fashion designer Kate Spade was so unfortunate. It was said she left a note addressed to her daughter that said "go and ask Dad what happened." A few months prior to her untimely passing, her husband had requested a divorce. Kate Spade was reportedly worth over four hundred million dollars. Her life was a testament to the strength of mothers and the fact that money doesn't define one's mental status. I asked myself what her purpose in life was? What was her happy place? What did she look forward to? Hearing her story broke my heart and it is my prayer that we hear less stories about women taking their lives and more about those who got the help that they needed in time to turn things around. May we forever be healed.

GOT PURPOSE?

IT IS MY hope that mothers and people in general will design a new purpose for their lives. If they get tired of the one they are currently working towards, it is my prayer that everyone will wake up trying to achieve an intended purpose in their life. There's so much to be done that no one should wake up without a purpose. You should be able to put your feet down and live. Every day you feel that you have accomplished anything towards your purpose is a day of celebration. Our purpose must not be rooted in material things but in the gifts and talents that we can give to the world.

We must learn to recognize the signs of mental health crises within ourselves and anyone that we can save from demise. From suicide prevention to preventative care, we are called to familiarize ourselves with information that empowers us to empower ourselves and others. We need more preventive care and more information. Change starts with our immediate community, and the time is now.

The act of caring for ourselves is directly connected to our mental health status. Engaging in opportunities to balance and center ourselves is heavily coveted as moments to maintain a fresh mental disposition. For many working mothers, self-care is limited to the occasional mani/pedi, or dinner without the kids. Self-care has so many attributes that we often fail to address the fullness of the concept and its associated benefits. Self-care is multi-dimensional in nature. We must go beyond the ongoing discussion of the physical perspective only as it relates to self-care. There are three components that encompass self-care and they are as follows: Mental, Spiritual and Physical.

Although often generated, there is no excuse good enough to pass on taking care of the vessels that we have been given. One major conflict that arises is time. So many working mothers and women in general believe that there are not enough hours in the day to care for themselves and others. Time is of the essence and we have a responsibility to be good stewards over the time that we have allotted. We all have the same twenty-four hours in the day. How we choose to spend that time is up to each of us. My equation for the use of time has proven to be reliable on many occasions.

Family Time	5 hours
Work	9 hours
Personal Time	2 hours
Sleep	8 hours

Another factor that is associated with the absence of self-care is the lack of money. Sound management of our finances is paramount for every other aspect of our lives and the homes that we build for our families. Taking care to establish self-care as a priority amongst the financial obligations that require immediate attention can ignite a trend that places your well-being at the forefront.

Establishing connections to the universe can bring about unspeakable peace. No matter what your religious beliefs are, it is imperative that we find a way to tap into a power higher than ourselves. Summoning a divine connection is most powerful when we align with the right people, places and things to produce positive vibes all around us. Recognizing instances in which your energy increases and decreases provides great insight as to where you should direct your focus. And for mothers who feel guilty about reserving time for self, I say to you, "relinquish the guilt". To fully give of yourself in a demanding capacity such as motherhood, you must first be whole. Engaging in activities to empower your mind prepares you to endure the trials and most importantly the triumphs of motherhood.

We all have wants, needs and desires and as different as we may seem, there are some things that we value that ring true for each of us. These desires cross all boundaries, including socioeconomic, racial, religious and any other divisory line that exists. We as a human race encompass a need to be heard and understood and fulfilled. I've narrowed down what we all want, need and deserve into five categories:

5 THINGS THAT EVERYONE DESIRES

1. FINANCIAL Freedom.
2. TO love and to be loved.
3. A career you enjoy.
4. HAPPINESS.
5. LIVE a life of purpose.

These five factors lead you to a state of wholeness and fulfillment that comes from within. It is extremely important that we continue to innovate ways to discover these five areas for sustained growth, development and mental stability.

MENTAL HEALTH FOR WOMEN OF COLOR

WHY HAS SOCIETY placed the burden of being strong on the shoulders of women of color?

From the beginning of time, women of color have personified the muscle of the culture. This is not to say that men don't embody strength, it is just allocated in different ways. There is a stigma attached to women of color that weakness is not permissible. We are expected to endure at all things, at all times. This disposition can be taxing mentally for many. Subscribing to this notion serves as a precursor to feelings of being overwhelmed as well as the need to sacrifice self to not let others down. When our self-worth is attached to our ability to be of service to others, as is the case for most mothers, then we experience feelings of inadequacy if we don't live up to standards superficially set for us.

And if by chance, we take the initiative to become transparent enough to share our moments of vulnerability, we are often told to "pray about it." As a Christian, I believe with my heart that there is unyielding power in the act of lifting our concerns and the deepest sentiments of our hearts up in prayer. I also believe that there can be no manifestation of miracles without action.

Why is it that it often feels as though our concerns are not heard? At what point are we allowed to be vulnerable? And if we are expected to help everyone, who shall help us?

It is my hope that we will continue to do the work of opening the lines of communication for all, and that we create platforms to ensure that our mental disposition is cared for and becomes a priority to others, just as the welfare of others is a priority to us. Women of color deserved to be preserved at all costs. As with every working mother, to have a sound mental capacity is to have a victory for all of the lives that we live to serve and protect.

I DON'T HAVE TIME!

STOP SAYING, "I don't have time; instead, say: "I have to manage my schedule better."

It's been a long time since I stepped foot into a physics class. But I still remember the first Law of Thermodynamics, which states that "energy (matter) can neither be created nor destroyed; it can only be transformed from one form to another."

That statement is not only true when finding "X" in a physics class, but also very applicable to the principle of life. Let's talk about time. We have twenty-four hours in a day, and no matter our circumstances, we cannot change that fact. We can not create more time in the day beyond the given twenty-four hours. We can however transform or reallocate the way we spend our time.

The human mind is also a very powerful tool. What we think and believe drives our actions. Does it make any sense to say "I don't have time to..." or "I don't have time for..."? I must then ask — "When will you have time?" There will still be twenty-four hours in a day when you wake up in the morning.

Each time you feel the need to say that you don't have time to carry on an important task, milestone, event, career move, family time, personal time, etc. Consider shifting your mind to think of ways that you can better manage your time and items on your schedule. Some questions to ask include: What's a must pay bill? What can wait? What's important? What's a 'just do it' task? What do I need vs what I want?

The best time to take that trip, start that business or make that career shift is now!

If you can breathe, you have time.

SIXTEEN
POSTPARTUM DEPRESSION

"Under no circumstances should any mother be ashamed of her story."
-Linda Arrey-

THERE ARE MANY subjects that we don't discuss enough, postpartum depression is one of them. The discussion is not happening often enough, especially in the black community. As someone who has suffered, I can attest to the fact that it is a very real condition.

Many women suffer in silence because people don't normalize it in the communities of people of color. Black women are left to deal with it internally. In many instances, it is not spoken of at all. I've heard women make traumatizing comments such as: "I hated my baby when he was born." A mother who is in a healthy state of mind would never speak this way. However, a mother who is amidst suffering would. When there is no support system, women aren't talking. When women aren't talking, there is no establishment of support assembled. If a mother asks for help, she should not be told to be strong or be denied.

A common theme among those suffering is a lack of interest in the things that once gave them gratification. Another factor is laughing less often. So many mothers feel less of who they used to be after having the baby. Sometimes, women need to heal, and sometimes, women need professional help. We must find ways to keep the lines of communication open and honest. A woman should not be ashamed to ask for help while suffering from postpartum depression.

After having my baby, there were days when I felt less than. I could talk to my husband about it, but there were times that I don't know if he took it seriously. It is hard for someone who is not certified to be of assistance. His listening ear was needed and necessary. I'm thankful that he was very receptive. When I saw my doctor, I talked her ear "off." She would talk, and talk and talk about my stresses. She didn't think I had postpartum depression; she thought that I had intense levels of stresses. After returning to work and taking care of my business, I was empowered to navigate life and to rediscover balance. I felt like I had been someone who was on the move, chasing my goals, and now, as a new mother, life looked completely different. I was not mentally or physically capable of doing all of the things that I had once done.

I was anxious about leaving my baby when I was required to travel for work. I knew that I was not under any circumstances when I left my child at home with a babysitter. I traveled with a nanny. Sometimes my nanny was even my sister. My little girl, Angel, traveled on so many planes. I had not spent one night without her since she was born. I don't think that's a good thing, but mentally I was not able to do it. Traveling with my child was not the healthiest thing either, and that's something I'm still dealing with. Separating anxiety, that has never left, is still very much a part of who I am. I'm so attached to my kids. I think that I should be able to spend a night without my children and be okay, but I'm not there yet.

One major challenge that we face as new mothers is accepting new dimensions for our bodies. I was a size zero prior to giving birth. Society has an unrealistic expectation of women to get right back into their pre-pregnancy bodies immediately after giving birth. I eat healthy and mostly African food, and I even like to work out. After giving birth, I did not snap back according to my plan. This is another challenge that a lot of women face. Social media and society lead us to believe that we should immediately resemble our pre-pregnancy weight. You just carried a baby for nine whole months, why would you be the same? What if we gave our bodies the same amount of time to adjust as we utilized to bring forth new life? To avoid feelings of depression and displeasure with ourselves, why don't we consider our old clothes to be motivation, as opposed to a source of hopelessness? We must teach mothers that there is no need to be stressed out about allowing their bodies to return to their original dimensions. We must learn to place greater emphasis on bonding with the babies who deserve all of our love and energy. Enjoy time with your child, work on proper breastfeeding and forget about the body image while you're creating this bond. I'm not saying that you should let your body go but don't make it your focus.

Don't put pressure on yourself to snapback. Enjoy being a mother, enjoy your child and don't fall into the pressure to be anything other than yourself.

Anxiety and postpartum depression go hand in hand. I can admit that with children, my anxiety levels have significantly increased. Having babies just changes you. From a mental, social and physical perspective, a mother is never the same after children. The hormone adjustments are another factor that we must consider. How could we not experience a shift? We are the givers of life, and we must attend to our emotional health. The livelihood of our families depends upon the stability that we can provide. We don't deserve to suffer from Postpartum depression in silence. We must come together and raise our voices to create awareness and to bring about positive change for the continued healing of our minds, bodies and souls.

SEVENTEEN
BREASTFEEDING

"A mother's love is nourishment
to her child's soul."
-Linda Arrey-

JUST BEFORE I had children, I always said that I would breastfeed. I began reading a great deal about the tremendous benefits, and I knew that it was something that I would commit to for my child. Growing up, our parents breastfed. Formula was always a second option. The women in my family supplemented where needed but breastfeeding was the primary option. When I was pregnant with Angel, I went to these breastfeeding sessions and I actually paid for them. After she was born, I wondered why I wasted my time and money. They don't prepare you; they were very superficial. I don't know if they just didn't want to scare new mothers, but I was not the better for having attended.

By the time my baby arrived, I was ill prepared. I thought I just had to grab my breast and let my child nurse. I had no idea how much went into the exchange and the logistics involved in the process. I had to make sure that she was properly latching on and that I was producing milk for her to be nurtured. I was mortified to learn that my baby had arrived, but I had no milk. She was unhappy because she was not fulfilled. The doctors assured me that she was getting all of the nutrients that she needed from colostrum and that she was maintaining the right amount of weight. I began to get increasingly worried. I recalled reading that, the milk might not arrive immediately. It is possible that in the days after the child is born, the milk has not yet arrived? On the second day, after my baby's birth, there was still no milk. My baby wanted to nurse. The doctors advised me to allow my baby to lay by the breast. By day number three, I woke up to the worst pain ever, coupled with a fever. My breasts felt like rocks, and I could not understand what was happening to me. My milk had arrived. Who could have prepared me for a moment such as that? No one prepares women for the reality. Breastfeeding is great but also very challenging. Breast milk is great for a baby's nutrition. The act of breastfeeding is also good for both mother and baby to bond. Among the many challenging aspects of breastfeeding, I was also ill. I knew nothing about what was happening to my body, and I was ill prepared for all of the changes that I was expecting. I wasn't even walking yet after my C-Section. My husband had to carry me to the shower so I could allow the steam to stimulate my milk to come down. Thank God for the arrival of my milk; my baby latched on.

Knowing what I know now, I don't believe that my baby was latching properly. I thought that if the nipple was in her mouth she would be nursing. But what is a proper latch? How much is the nipple supposed to be in the mouth? How far are her lips supposed to be on the nipple? I was in so much pain that my nipples actually chipped from breastfeeding. Based on her weight, my body was producing enough to meet my daughter's demand. It takes time for your body to adjust. It doesn't happen overnight. It's important for women to understand this. No one told me that breastfeeding was a journey that required patience. My daughter wasn't latching on properly, which caused me concern. You have to let the baby latch on, even when you don't think the milk is coming. You have to be consistent until you and the baby establish a relationship of what she needs. The most important attribute for breastfeeding success is being determined. If you're not determined, those first two weeks will prove to be more challenging than one can handle.

I can understand why almost half of new moms opt not to breastfeed. When times get increasingly difficult, just wanting to breastfeed is not enough. You have to want it because you know that it's what is best for your child. What worked well for me is setting milestones. The good news is that if you can get past the first couple of weeks, you will surpass the first milestone. Breastfeeding for two months was my next milestone. People will give you so much advice and even pressure you to give your baby formula. You might be forced to consider it because you don't want your baby to suffer from hunger. Tell people in your circle that the best thing that they can do to help you is to encourage you.

One of my girlfriends who had a baby a year older than my daughter was also a breastfeeding mother. It was good to find someone who was walking along the same path that I was. I encourage mothers to become a part of a support system or find and join a group in your area of residence. I was living in Columbus, Mississippi at the time. Although they had Le Leche League, most of their meetings were hosted during working hours, so I was unable to get involved. If I could have attended a support group, I would have.

When it comes to breastfeeding, you have to build a relationship with your body so that it establishes what it should be producing for your baby. I would have to wake up late at night to pump, because that supply and demand system is a real concept. During my first pregnancy, I would be sitting at work and then my breasts would start leaking. This could have been in part because I started pumping too early. It seemed as if my body was always leaking milk. For mothers returning to work, it's good to have a stash. You also don't need a freezer full of milk, unless you have a job that doesn't allow you time to express. There are state regulations that require jobs to allow lactating time and stations to do so. Check company policies for adherence to the lactation stations and local policies. Gone are the days when women are forced to breastfeed on the toilet seat in the public restroom, while missing their lunch break. I breastfed Angel and Ariel for a full year both times around because I was pumping milk for the next day, while at work. You have to be consistent. I know a lot of people who say you're more effective if you pump every three hours; I pumped twice a day while in the office. A lot of times when women have freezers full of milk, they still have that milk when they're not breastfeeding. If you nurse and you want to pump after, understand that you're probably going to over produce. I just want the women who don't have that freezer stash to not worry about it. You will produce enough. Over time, I gained more confidence as a breastfeeding mother. I started perfecting my lactation skills.

My second time around breastfeeding, our daughter Ariel was seamless. We both established a breastfeeding routine early on. I didn't begin pumping, until it was time to return to work, which meant that I never had any concerns with overflow or leakage.

Today, as a mother of two, I can recognize the similarities and differences in their nursing patterns. My first born loved to nurse for long periods of time, because she would sit on the breast for two to three hours. Even when I ran out of milk, she would continue to nurse for comfort. Comfort nursing is another way to produce more milk. If your baby does not want to comfort nurse, then consider pumping after nursing. After I returned to work, I communicated with my boss that I was nursing and needed time to pump. I informed him that I would be shutting my door at designated times. It's good to communicate with your team so they know that you will be taking these intervals in the day to pump. I highly recommend the hands-free pump, which allows you to complete other tasks. I must admit that pumping has evolved as my most productive time of my day.

When it comes to formula, I want everyone to recognize it as an option. Some women feel it is the end of the world to not breastfeed. It is not the end of the world. In most cases, mothers who have a desire to breastfeed need to simply free their minds and relax. Stressing about milkflow is counterproductive. One of the ways to relax is knowing there are other options.

Formula is not a bad thing. Formula fed babies turn out just fine. We are told that breast milk produces antibodies and that breastfed babies will be more resistant to germs, but trust me, when my daughter went to daycare she still came home with a cold. Breast milk has a lot of nutrients, but formula has been cultivated so that it is so similar to breast milk.

If breastfeeding doesn't work, then formula is the next best thing. If you don't want to breastfeed, that's fine, no one should judge you. It's a personal thing and it's challenging. As I talk about postpartum depression, I recognize that breastfeeding can affect women in different ways. It might cause aggravation or comfort from the opportunity to bond. It may relieve a mother from the effects of postpartum. The bottom line is that you must know what works for you. People shame people who are formula feeding and praise those who breastfeed. We shouldn't shame any mother for caring for her child. That's the reason why so many women choose to breastfeed not because they want to, but because they want the medal. The choice to decide what is right for you and your baby should be yours. If breastfeeding works for you, go for it. If not, be proud and own it.

Don't do it to tell the world. Don't do it because your neighbor is doing it. Do what works best for you.

You are the best mom your child will ever have. Your child knows that you love them and that you are doing the best that you can to make sure that they get the best. Learn to relax. The reason we're not being productive is because we are too stressed over things we have no control over. If you have exhausted all the options and you did the best you could in an attempt to breastfeed, exploring options such as taking lactation pills or trying supplements and you aren't producing the milk, do not starve your child. The most important thing is that your child is healthy. You have to do what is best for your child. Understand that it is not about you at this point. It's about you taking care of your child. Feel confident that there is no one that is going to love this child that you have carried for nine months more than you. Your child is the first one that heard your heartbeat from inside of you. When you hold your baby, while giving them a meal, they will recognize that same heartbeat. They will recognize your love. You will not let your child down.

In 2016, I held a conference in Washington, D.C. as a way to advocate for breastfeeding. I wanted to establish a forum for women who were struggling with breastfeeding to discuss the issues and to establish a basis of support. I was astounded by the tremendous scores of women who were in attendance. I actually received an award for hosting the event. We gave out breast pumps to ten women. It's definitely a topic that is near and dear to my heart. I want women to hear and understand that they can realize the benefits of breastfeeding for their children. I have overheard things that don't quite add up such as, "I'm not going to breastfeed because I want to live my life." Maybe it doesn't add up to me because it is not my personal choice, but let's be clear, breastfeeding is not the end of your social life. Maybe you have to be more selective with your outings, and outfits, but that's about where it ends. I used to be the type of girl who asked for people's permission to breastfeed in public places? That girl is no more. My baby has to eat, and I will not compromise feeding my baby's need to eat for a stranger's comfort. If someone is uncomfortable with a breastfeeding mother, then they should exit to the left. You may be slightly inconvenienced but never out of options.

Additionally, it is important to note that there are several clothing lines that design for breastfeeding mothers. If you're not the bold type, get a blanket and place it over your shoulder to cover you and the baby. You don't have to lose yourself to breastfeed. That's another reason why I've heard people say "no." I have a friend who stated that she wanted to go on vacation, so she stopped breastfeeding. I advised her to pump while she was gone and ship the milk back home using dry ice.

I can honestly say that society is doing a much better job at praising women for breastfeeding. Breastfeeding is a lifestyle that commands impressive benefits for both mother and child. The opportunity to do so is one that should not be taken for granted. Why not give your children the world?

EIGHTEEN
FIBROIDS

"I give thanks for every opportunity masked as a struggle."
-Linda Arrey-

FIBROIDS HAS BECOME a health concern that we cannot afford to deny. We must open the lines of communication and leave no stone unturned to ensure our safety. As a woman, I accept responsibility for educating and healing women who suffer in silence from the presence of fibroids. The reality is that women don't know they have fibroids until symptoms reveal themselves. It is imperative that we learn to listen to and understand our bodies. We must not shy away from being checked, especially as we approach thirty. A lot of change comes with that age. Creating a culture in which we are prepared to implement early detection measures is urgent. By the time we turn thirty years of age, our bodies experience profound transformations. Detection is critical.

DETECTION. DIAGNOSIS. TREATMENT.

I WAS THIRTY when I found out that I had fibroids. I suddenly experienced a lot of heavy bleeding during my periods and severe back pain. Sometimes the pain was so intense that I could not walk. There were days that by the time I got into a car to drive to work, I was having to run to the bathroom to change my sanitary pad. My fibroids were detected through an ultrasound. To be certain, the doctor ordered a CT scan. When the CT scan came back, it was confirmed that I had five fibroids, with the largest being five cm. Most fibroids are usually benign, but even so, my doctor, recommended surgery. She advised me to get them taken out before I get pregnant. During that time, my husband and I were talking about starting a family. There were many occasions that the pelvic pain, pressure, and heavy, long periods were unbearable. Upon conceiving our first child, things changed. When pregnancy kicked in and the periods stopped I felt an uncanny sense of relief. I was thrilled at the prospect of not having a period for the next nine months. Contrary to what I believed, that really wasn't the case. As my baby progressed, the blood vessels that were feeding my baby were also feeding the fibroids. Over time, the fibroids got bigger and the pain became worse. I started going in to the doctor's office more frequently. The plan was for them to keep monitoring me in an attempt to keep the baby from harm's way. The baby progressed and the fibroids continued to grow.

    I remember vividly the morning I woke up in excruciating pain and walked myself to the hospital. While at the ER, the staff paged my OB/GYN. She had advised me to call the hospital if I had any concerns. The doctor happened to be at a nearby city when everything unfolded, but responded to the call. To my recollection, she was not on call that day. Many medical professionals don't often demonstrate their acknowledgement of the fact that there is power in the relationships build with the patients. For Dr. Lacy, it was never about the money. She genuinely cares about her patients.

I trusted her and that she had my best interests at heart. As she entered the room with her usual friendly smile, the first words out of her mouth were: "Oh God, is the baby coming?" I told her everything that had been going on. The hospital staff didn't know if I was in labor. They stated that it appeared as if I was dilated.

Considering I may be in labor, she advised me that they may have to turn me upside down to clip my cervix. At twenty four weeks into my pregnancy, I was faced with the possibility that I may be having my baby early. After examining me, the doctor informed me that they will not be clipping my cervix after all. The baby wasn't coming. What they were feeling was a large fibroid, not the baby's head. One of the fibroids had gotten so big that it was blocking my cervix

I was given pain meds while at the hospital and monitored for two days. On day two, my doctor said to me, "I got news for you, woman. You are not going back to work. You need to be on bed rest." In my mine at the time, that was the worst news that I could have been told that early into my pregnancy. "What will I be doing for the remaining four months before the baby comes?" I wondered. After being discharged to go home, I was in a lot of pain which prevented me from walking on my own. I was blessed to have my brother who was visiting stay with me for a few weeks.

There were times that I went against the doctor's recommendation and attempted to work. Being told I couldn't work put me in a depressive state. I was a workaholic for lack of a better word. I kept calling my team, and sharing updates. Gradually I started realizing that my focus needed to be on taking care of myself and the well-being of our unborn child. The notion of working for fulfillment was really just me trying to fill the void of the emptiness I was feeling.

It was during these quiet moments that I realized I didn't want to write a book that focused only on business; rather I wanted to write a book that spoke to my daughters about different aspects of life.

I was in a new space mentally and spiritually. The moment I accepted my new faith of rest, self-care and rejuvenation, I began implementing a mindset shift and loving the slow pace and quiet time. I still missed going to work, but it slowly became none of my worry. I prayed for a healthy baby, sang to her, talked to her and listened to her every move, including the hiccups. I started enjoying staying up late with no worry of waking up early in the morning. I also caught up on trash TV— yes, I watch that too. The beauty about keeping a nine to five job, especially serving in the military is that I remained gainfully employed. Money wasn't an issue.

I had a total of five Fibroids. At one point one of them was bigger than my baby's head. The doctors were concerned that the fibroid was getting too big, such that the baby didn't have enough room. I also became a C-section candidate, because it was too risky to push a baby through a fibroid. Come delivery day, I had prepared my mind for any outcome. The doctor said that there would be two surgeons in the room during the delivery because they would try to take the fibroids out, along with the baby. They also had pints of blood in the room because during a C-section, you lose a lot of blood. All of the doctors in the room knew their role. My doctor would take care of the baby, and the other doctor would attend to the fibroids.

Upon administering the epidural, they had to poke me a couple of times. He kept missing the spot on my spine, and that wasn't fun. When a C-section is being conducted, you hear everything. Zofran and having

Tse by my side comforting me saved the day. I was extremely nauseous and felt as though I was going to puke. While laying there, you're just praying to hear your baby cry. You can see the medical staff pulling your stomach out but there's no pain. You feel a great deal of pressure. They detected the presence of twelve fibroids, not five as initially stated. I could hear the doctors say that they are unable to take them out because if they did, there's the possibility of bleeding to death. Finally, after much anticipation, there was a cry. It was the most beautiful sound that I had ever heard. There is nothing better than that sound other than when I heard it for the second time with our second Princess. As they prepared to take the baby out of the room, I asked to hold her while they stitched me up with all 12 Fibroids. The delivery was a success. When I finally got to the room, it was apparent that I had lost a lot blood. I was weak.

They came and gave me two pints of blood. I was told that I could schedule another surgery to remove the fibroids. That was up for consideration for when I recovered from the c-section. After the pregnancy, the fibroids reduced in size, and I was okay with that. Ten months later, I discovered that we were pregnant again.

The fight against Fibroids was reinstated. My doctor advised me that I was a candidate for a Vaginal Birth After Cesarean (VBAC). Five months into my second pregnancy, the offer for VBAC was rescinded due to health concerns. By the grace of God, I was able to work up to thirty eight weeks the second time around. My body was once again reinforcing the fact that I needed to take rest. I took bed rest again, to prepare for the baby. By the time the delivery day arrived, we were ready. We thanked God once again as we welcomed our second Princess, Ariel. I have been blessed with two successful pregnancies and two of God's greatest creations, my daughters. The fibroids struggle is not yet a story of the past.

WEIGHING THE OPTIONS

WHEN YOU EXPERIENCE discomfort, you must listen to your body. It is equally important to use the process of elimination to either eliminate fibroids or to receive a diagnosis.

Some women are able to manage their systems or maybe implement a lifestyle change. We must determine the best options for treatment. Either way, it is important to empower yourself with knowledge.

Speaking with a doctor about the various options for treatment as well as what considerations need to be addressed is critical. An Intrauterine Device (IUD) can serve as a symptomatic treatment for some women. This is a current option for me. I have to admit, I was not considering the fibroids when I had mine inserted. My main concern was not getting pregnant again so soon.

I was happy to discover that this one device could solve two problems.

The Office of Women's Health reports that birth control is an option to decrease the impact of the symptoms. For people with severe symptoms, doctors might recommend surgeries. A hysterectomy is an option for those who don't want anymore children or those who don't have the desire of having children. In these instances, the uterus is removed as to not allow opportunity for the fibroids to return. Another procedure is called MyoSure. This procedure removes intrauterine tissue that can include polyps and fibroids.

The important thing to keep in mind is that there are options.

There is another procedure where they burn the source of the fibroids, dependent on how symptomatic you are and your tolerance levels. As a woman suffering from fibroids, the most important action that you can take before making a decision, is to talk to your doctor and to know your body. It is imperative that you are empowered to make informed decisions.

YOU ARE NOT ALONE

STATISTICS DOCUMENT THAT twenty-one million women live with fibroids. This is an epidemic. To date, there is little to no research on what causes Fibroids. It is imperative that we have this conversation to create much needed awareness. Currently, there is little to no funding for the research of fibroids. We need medical industry professionals to invest time to find out more information that can lead to advocacy and preventative care. We must stand twenty-one million strong and tell our stories, so that women will not suffer in silence. We must learn to listen to our bodies so that we can be the first line of detection. We must learn to arm ourselves with information. If you are having symptomatic periods, such as irregularities, painful or heavy periods, talk to your doctor, be in the know and discuss your options. You don't have to live with pain that is unbearable. There are options.

I am an advocate because I want for us to open the lines of communication and discuss this epidemic that is so devastating. We must talk about it. If you have painful periods, I encourage you to dig deeper. What is causing the painful periods? Talk to a doctor! Don't ignore symptoms such as heavy bleeding, blood clots, or pelvic pain. These could be signals for fibroids. It is imperative that you seek medical attention and eliminate all possibilities.

I was having a conversation with a few of my colleagues. The group was composed of two women and one man. I was sharing various aspects of this book with them. I also explained that I had the intention to address the topic of fibroids. No one on that table was familiar with fibroids. The people with whom I spoke were degreed and are medical professionals. Their unfamiliarity was shocking to me. It was also confirmation that this work to serve as a voice for so many women suffering in silence is not in vain.

To learn more about fibroids, please visit any of the resources below. The life you save, could be your own:

Uterine fibroids." Office on Women's Health, U.S. Department of Health and Human Services. February 6, 2017. https://www.womenshealth.gov/a-z-topics/uterine-fibroids#a

About Uterine Fibroids." Center for Uterine Fibroids, Brigham and Women's Hospital. http://www.fibroids.net/fibroids.html

Uterine fibroids, Symptoms and causes." Mayo Clinic. July 6, 2016. http://www.mayoclinic.org/diseases-conditions/uterine-fibroids/symptoms-causes/dxc-20212514

NINETEEN
THE SILENT FEAR

"I carried you every second of your life."
-Linda Arrey-

AROUND MY FIFTH week of pregnancy, the silent fear was instilled in me that I will never forget. I carried the words of despair that a nurse had spoken to me throughout the duration of my pregnancy. Once you get pregnant in the military, you have to ensure that your pregnancy is documented in the system to be placed on a non-deployable profile. I had to go to the civilian sector to see an OB/GYN, but the doctor I wanted to see was booked. I told the nurse that I was a returning patient and that I was five weeks pregnant. I was told that I couldn't be seen until I was eight weeks pregnant. The nurse who booked the appointment told me not to get too excited about the pregnancy. She added that the first eight weeks would be a period of waiting, because many miscarriages occur within this period of time. Although she may have been doing her job, her words hung over my head like a cloud. I was nervous, stressed and anxious to celebrate the joy of bringing a new life forward. Admittedly, I was overwhelmed with fear. Instead of erasing her words from my psyche after I crossed the first of many finish lines at eight weeks, they continued to become a part of what I thought about every day.

In the midst of your pregnancy, you might think that you are the only mother who fears miscarriage, but the truth is that we are all thinking about it. Miscarriage is more common than we know, because we often don't speak on it. When you get pregnant, you think that the nine months will pass quickly, and then a baby will be born. To think this way is hardly realistic. A full term pregnancy feels like forever.

I want to encourage mothers awaiting the arrival of their babies to remain confident that all will be well. And while we can not pretend that miscarriage is not a real thing, we can remain confident in knowing that our bodies are constructed to give birth and bring forth life.

We might not all be successful in carrying our babies to full term, but we must continue to place our hopes and faith in the Lord, who is the giver of life. This silent fear will sometimes make its unfortunate presence known, but we are all successful in being worthy of our contributions to the world. We deserve to remember that we matter, regardless of the shape or form that motherhood takes in our lives. To all of the mothers that have suffered the loss of a baby, may you stay encouraged and remember that you are forever loved.

TWENTY
THE LAW OF ATTRACTION

"As she envisions herself living in abundance, she attracts more."
-Linda Arrey-

IT'S TRUE THAT your vibe attracts your tribe. The energy that you radiate attracts similar energy. The Law of Attraction starts within us. It begins with the way in which we treat people and the way in which we want to be treated. When you are for people you want them to be for you. It is important that we wake up each morning and set precedents to see what can be done to make everyone's day better. As humans, we are naturally selfish. We often consider what others can do for us? In this state, we end up missing out on our blessings. When we spend time trying to figure out how we can be served as opposed to being of service, we don't win in abundance.

If we approach life with a giving perspective, our hands are open and ready to receive. It's not just in tangible items but also in our time and our attitude. If you're channeling love and happiness and positivity, it will surely come back to you. The moment I walk into my kids' classroom, after having a bad day, and they see me and just smile, everything goes away. Just imagine if we had that effect on everyone we encountered. What if we resolved to brighten everyone's day instantly? It is possible to create an aura that makes everyone want to be in your space and want to be their best by your presence. In the workplace, if you want people to do for you what you expect, you have to show that you care and that everybody is a contributor to the team. You must not establish the element of dictatorship in your space. To be a good leader you have to be a good follower. Show your team members that you can be part of a team. Work to understand the needs of others. When your staff and people around you don't feel that you have a genuine concern for their well being, they will not give you their best. It is really simple. We must radiate the same energy that we want channeled back to us. Carry yourself with confidence, be kind to everyone, be polite and respectful. Above all else, channel love. Change your perspective and the way you treat people. By just the way you carry yourself, the way you treat other people, and the way that you talk will show people that your intent is to attract positive energy.

10 PRINCIPLES TO LIVE RIGHT

1. FOCUS on Your Goals
2. ANALYZE Progress
3. CELEBRATE Small Victories
4. DISCOVER Your Truth
5. BE Kind to Yourself and Others
6. CHALLENGE Yourself To Learn New Things
7. SILENCE Complaints and Distractions
8. HAVE a Positive Mindset
9. CHASE A Dream
10. LIVE Faith Based

CONCLUSIVE THOUGHT
A Four Letter Word

Love

Is

A

Word

CAVEAT
BE THE LIGHT

"And in darkness, a mother becomes the light."
-Linda Arrey-

IF NO ONE has told you today, you are appreciated. You make the decision each and every day to put the needs of others in front of yours. For this reason alone, you are worthy to be praised. There is so much inside of you that has not yet escaped. I challenge you to launch out and pursue your dreams. I challenge you to trust your ideas and abilities. The time for you to turn your thoughts into action is now. You have dedicated so much to others, it's now your time to shine.

IV.
EPILOGUE: THE JOYS OF MOTHERHOOD

*"This joy I have, is unspeakable.
God gave me a piece of myself
when he made me a mother."*
—Linda Arrey—

LOVE MY KIDS in a way that is unexplainable. It is without question that I love my husband dearly. The love that I have for them does not compare. It is like comparing oranges and plums. I don't have the capacity to compare the two. I honor and love them both. They are not in the same category. As mothers, we must not be shy about loving our kids. Doing so doesn't make our husbands less valuable. I honor and value marriage. I honor and value family. The greatest joy in my heart was established with and through my family. They are so important to me.

My children changed my heart. They made me appreciate life itself. After becoming a mother, I had a new zest for simple luxuries, like the sun and the moon and the stars. I appreciate everything about life and now have a deeper sense of living. As I compose the pages of this book, I'm nursing my baby. Moments such as these, when I am just holding her right here close to me is proof that there is joy in motherhood. My Friday nights have not been the same, since becoming a mother. I only desire to spend time in the rapture of love that my family offers. Listening to their laughs and seeing their smiles encourages me to be all that I can.

The joys of motherhood are remembering the immense feelings of love inside your heart. The joys of motherhood allows you to rediscover all that is good in the world. Most importantly, the joys of motherhood lead you towards the most powerful act that you can engage in, LOVE.

It is my hope that you will discover this same joy I have buried deep inside my soul.

V.
DEAR WORKING MOTHER

DEAR WORKING MOTHER,
LOVE is a four letter word that encompasses so many feelings. I began journaling to share my greatest emotions and to channel all of the emotions that motherhood ignited inside of me. My journal entries have become the foundation for this book. It is my greatest prayer that ever working mother will come to recognize her value and her worth. May God bless all that you touch. I wrote this book and these entries with love in my heart.

JUNE 28, 2016: HEALED BY AN ANGEL

MY DAUGHTER, MY Angel, healed me. Sleepless nights are no stranger to any mother, but we do it graciously night after night, whether in ill health or in perfect health. Last night I was in severe abdominal pain and struggled through the night. When my daughter, my Angel, woke up for her nightly feed and diaper change, mommy woke up graciously to attend to her precious jewel. It was a struggle to wake up through that pain, but I did it for my daughter. Then came time for nursing. I only used the traditional hold method to nurse my baby. As you know, it's not the most comfortable with abdominal pain. As you remember, I had a C-section, but she looked at me and smiled after her hungry cry. That heart melting smiling was all I needed. As I nursed my angel back to sleep, I realized not only did I feel fulfilled but that burning pain that cut through my lower abdomen subsided. I thought I was taking care of my daughter meanwhile the whole time she was taking care of me. My angel healed me.

OCTOBER 4, 2016: ANGEL TURNS SIX MONTHS

AS I LAY my daughter's outfit for school this morning, I am filled with gratitude. I am thankful that the lord trust Tse and I to raise our Angel, Our most precious gift. This day 6 months ago I went under the knife successfully and the result was not only the birth of our daughter but the rebirth of the woman I became. Thank you for teaching me patience, fulfilling my days with joy and laughter, and for introducing me to this unexplainable endless love. I pray that the Lord continues to guide Tse and I to raise you to His will. I love you with every fiber of my being.

Love, Mommy.

NOVEMBER 17, 2017: ARIEL TURNS TWO MONTHS

DEAR ARIEL, MY second Princess. You turned two months today. You are filled with vibrance and so much personality. Yet calm. With a clean diaper and full stomach one can't tell that there's a baby in the room. You bring us much joy and complete our family. Your big sister, Angel, also loves you so much. You bring her much joy and excitment. A part of me wants to say, "slow down Princess, don't grow up too fast on me," but I know you also desire to be able to play with your sister soon. We love you endlessly. Thank you for bringing us all so much joy.

Love Mummy

VI.
EXECUTING YOUR GOALS

SETTING GOALS IS important, but an unaccomplished goal is as good as not making any. Here are three words I have used to achieve my goals repeatedly, and how you can implement them to attain success.

Before we dive in, let me first emphasize the importance of writing your goals down. When you have a goal, write it down. The human mind is more committed to things that can be seen than our mare thoughts. I'm not asking that you make a billboard out of your goals. I simply advise that you write it down somewhere, even if you don't have plans of sharing with anyone, yet.

In the space below, write down three personal or professional goals that will transform your life once accomplished. These might be goals you have had in mind, but have never truly committed to them. Take the first step towards making a commitment now, by writing them down. Secondly, include expected completion dates for each goal. Aligning your goals with timelines helps you rate your progress and completion rates.

1. _____
   - I will complete by_____
2. _____
   - I will complete by_____
3. _____
   - I will complete by_____

Now that you have your goals written down:

BE DETERMINED

Make a firm decision about working on at least one goal each day, every day. Make a secondary list on what you need and the people you need in your circle execute each goal. Go through your list daily and attack at least one thing on each list. It may simply be sending out an email to a potential sponsor, sending a speaker request, working on your business plan, etc. Do at the minimum one thing daily. Also note that you don't have to work on all three goals simultaneously if they are very unrelated. You can commit to the most important goal on your list, the one that has the most impact towards transforming your life and commit to it. Once you have attained desired results, move to the next goal. An interesting fact is that often, when you accomplish your most valuable goal, everything else falls in place. Whether you make the decision to work on each goal concurrently or one goal at a time, make a firm decision to do so daily and unwaveringly.

BE INTENTIONAL

The productive way to get desired results is to align your purpose and passion with your skills. When you do something you are great at, and also have the passion for, you become unstoppable. Your skills will get things done, but it is your purpose and passion that will take you through those days that you feel defeated and want to give up. Aligning your skills, purpose and passion provides the motivation and intentions needed to keep moving one step forward towards accomplishing your goals.

BE CONSISTENT

To be effective and take your goals to the finish line, where you see and experience the transformation you desire, you have to be consistent with your execution. Make a conscious decision to follow through. Do what you say you would do. Meet promises to your clients, with your number one client being yourself. If you have a schedule stick with it. And when that schedule no longer serves you, make changes, then stick with the new schedule. It could be something as simple as consistency with your social media accounts, live videos or blogs. People notice when you are consistent and that helps build your credibility and brand.

Implementing these three words in my goal setting strategy has helped me tremendously accomplish my goals repeatedly, one of which was writing this book. I must add that I also meditate and pray over my goals. Before I go to bed each night, I acknowledge what I accomplished that day and pray over my list of 'to-dos' for the next day.

VII.
TAKE THE #21DAYWORKINGMOTHER CHALLENGE

Every woman has a story to tell. A great place to start is by writing your thoughts down. For the next twenty-one days, you are officially challenged to share your intimate thoughts and sentiments about all things motherhood. Use the space provided below.

DAY 1: WHAT IS THE BEST PARENTING ADVICE YOU HAVE RECEIVED?

DAY 2: SHARE YOUR FUNNIEST MOMENT WHEN THE KIDS WERE TOO QUIET.

DAY 3: WHAT DO YOU REMEMBER MOST ABOUT GIVING BIRTH?

DAY 4: WHAT IS THE ONE LESSON THAT YOU WANT YOUR CHILDREN TO ALWAYS REMEMBER?

DAY 5: SHARE YOUR PARENTING MANTRA.

DAY 6: IF YOU WERE TO WRITE A BOOK, WHAT WILL THE TITLE BE, AND WHAT WILL THE BOOK BE ABOUT?

DAY 7: DESCRIBE WHAT MAKES YOU HAPPY.

DAY 8: WHAT ARE SOME LIFESTYLE CHANGES YOU HAVE MADE SINCE BECOMING A MOTHER?

DAY 9: WHOM DO YOU TURN TO WHEN YOU NEED HELP?

DAY 10: AS A PARENT, HOW DO YOU WANT TO BE REMEMBERED?

DAY 11: GIVE ONE PARENTING MOMENT THAT YOU WISH YOU COULD BE GRANTED A "DO OVER."

DAY 12: WHAT DO YOU LOVE THE MOST ABOUT YOUR CHILDREN?

DAY 13: HOW DOES WORK MAKE YOU A BETTER PARENT?

DAY 14: HOW DOES PARENTING MAKE YOU A BETTER PROFESSIONAL?

DAY 15: DESCRIBE THE MOST DIFFICULT PARENT MOMENT THAT YOU HAVE EXPERIENCED.

DAY 16: WHAT INSPIRES YOU?

DAY 17: HOW DO YOU TEACH YOUR FAMILY ABOUT SPIRITUALITY?

DAY 18: WHAT IS YOUR SELF-CARE RITUAL?

DAY 19: DESCRIBE SOMETHING THAT YOU GIVE TO YOUR FAMILY THAT MONEY CAN'T BUY.

DAY 20: HOW DO YOU DEFINE BALANCE?

DAY 21: WHAT ARE YOU MOST GRATEFUL FOR?

Dear Reader,

IF YOU HAVE made it to the end of this, congratulations are in order! When we take a moment from our day to channel our thoughts and feelings in a progressive manner, transformation happens. The good news is that you don't have to stop here. I encourage you to join the #MEMOIRSOFAWORKINGMOTHER Facebook group (https://Facebook.com/groups/memoirsofaworkingmother) and connect with other like-minded mothers. Let's all learn, grow and get inspired together!

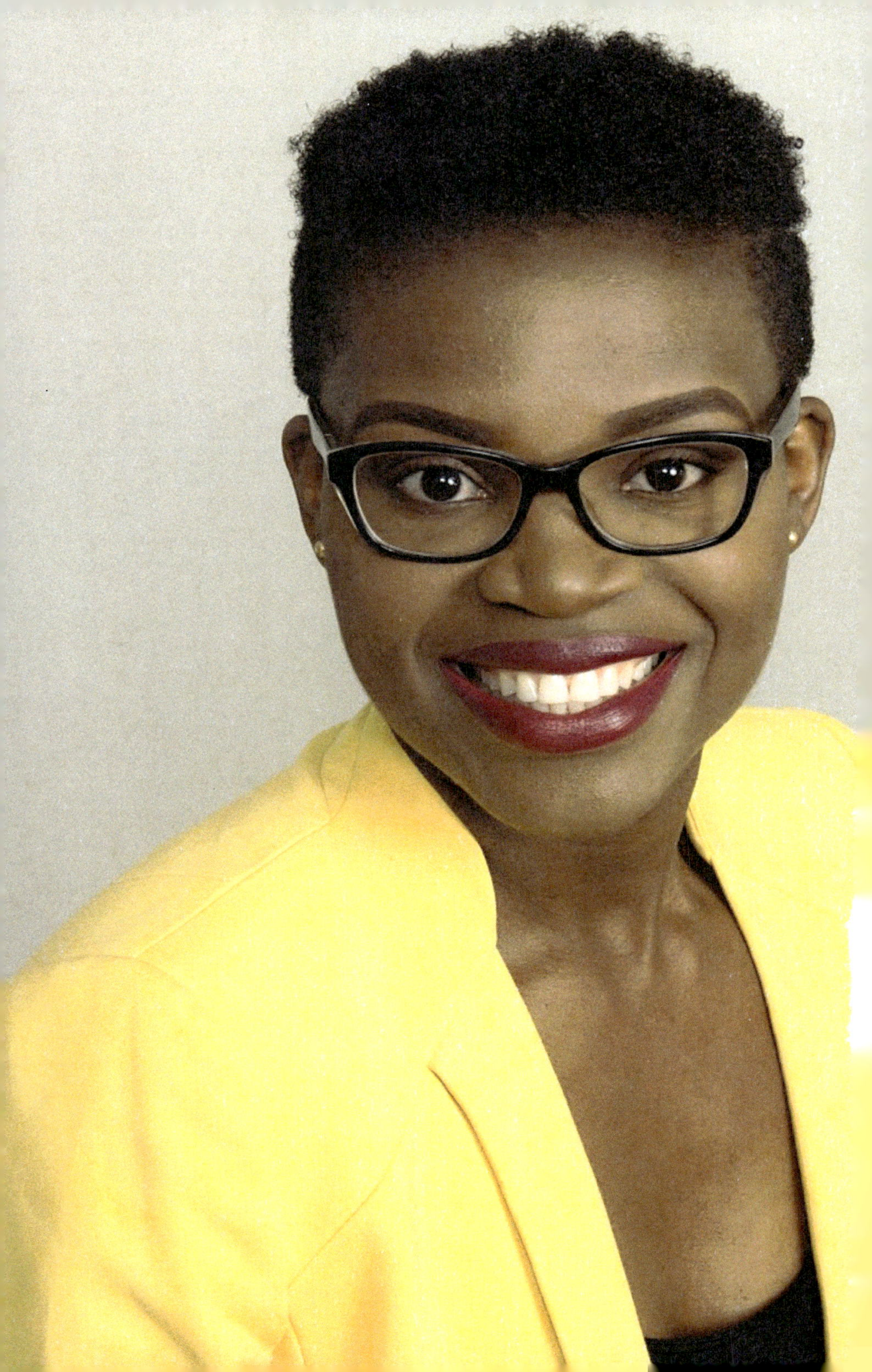

MEET AND CONNECT
with Linda Arrey

MRS. LINDA ARREY-MBI Nkwenti (best known as Linda Arrey) is an Author, Certified Life and Leadership Coach, Philanthropist and Speaker. She is the Founder and President of Women in Leadership Development and Empowerment, INC., (WILDE), a philanthropic organization of professional women from diverse backgrounds birth from Linda's vision and dedication to the education and empowerment of women globally and her inclination to improving individual and community standards. Coach Linda is constantly seeking innovative ways to give back to the community through mobilization, direct service, donations, and more. She is transforming lives by equipping working mothers to use their God-given talents to up-level both personally and professionally by finding CLARITY, implementing STRUCTURE and establishing an execution STRATEGY.

Upon becoming a mother, she has long advocated for the discovery of balance and compassion for working mothers thriving at home and in the workplace. Coach Linda is on a mission to help working mothers live their best lives.

"No working mother should work tirelessly, yet fail to enjoy the life and loved ones she continuously works for."

Her recent book, "Memoirs of a Working Mother," reveals the challenges and triumphs of returning to work after childbirth, battling with fibroids, finding balance with family and above all else, the quest to love the reflection in the mirror through a robust offering of stories, strategies, and anecdotes.

She holds a Master of Science in Healthcare Administration and Business. Among other community and professional organizations, she is a member of the American College of Healthcare Executives and the NGO Committee on the Status of Women Globally. She is a Captain in the United States Air Force Medical

Service Corps, currently serving as the Chief Information Officer at the 436th Medical Group. She is also a member of Academy Women, a world class professional development organization for military women and veterans.

"When I'm not coaching, speaking or fulfilling my military duties you can find me in my most valuable roles – Wife to Tse and Mother to two of God's greatest creations, my daughters. I enjoy family time, cooking, spending time at the beach, shopping online and traveling the world. Most importantly, I love the Lord"

– Coach Linda

CONNECT
WITH LINDA ARREY

Linda Arrey Global, LLC
Facebook/Instagram
https://Facebook.com/groups/memoirsofaworkingmother
@memoirsofaworkingmother
@coachlindaspeaks
@LindaArrey

LinkedIn
www.linkedin.com/in/lindaarrey

Website
www.LindaArrey.com

Email
LifeCoach@LindaArrey.com

Are You Feeling Stuck?

DO YOU DESIRE to maximize your full potential, tap into your God-given talents, elevate your life and career to the next level and live your best life?

If you answered "yes" to any of the above questions, I can help.

Hello, I am Coach Linda. I am a Wife to my loving husband, Tse and Mother to two gorgeous Princesses. Family is my priority and I am sure yours also. I have been in the business of empowering women for 14 years and one thing I take very seriously is coaching women to succeed personally and professional, both in the home and at the workplace.

I understand how confusing and challenging life may be when you are trying to accomplish goals solo. Living your best life begins with taking the right steps. It is not by chance that you are on my page.

I work with working mothers and female entrepreneurs in varying stages of their journeys by tapping into their full potential and God-given abilities to identify and walk in their purpose, attain balance and flexibility, scale their businesses, up-level and live life to the fullest.

As your Coach I am your partner in personal and professional growth. I work with you to live your full potential and attain desired results as follows:

Planning and Goal Setting: I work with you to create an effective plan with greater results. We will develop executable goals that cater to your areas of need and areas of improvement with an outcome to transform your life both personally and professionally, be more productive at home and in the workplace, while maximizing and monetizing your skills.

Managing Progress and Accountability: During our weekly calls or meetups, we will focus on what is important and ensure that you stay on track on courses of action we both agree on. We will make adjustments along the way as you accomplish your goals.

Finish Line: As your partner in personal and professional development, working together will make you accomplish your goals faster and I will ride with you to the finish line while celebrating accomplishments along the way.

TO SCHEDULE YOUR FREE ASSESSMENT CALL, PLEASE VISIT:

WWW.LINDAARREY.COM